"In this bracing *cri de coeu[r]* [...] lies and obfuscations to loca.. .... and racism. Marshaling compelling historical and theological evidence, *The Anti-Greed Gospel* presents a searing critique of the status quo and points Christians to a redemptive path forward. A must-read book for the American church."

—**Kristin Kobes Du Mez,** *New York Times* bestselling author of *Jesus and John Wayne*

"Many people say that the original sin of the United States was racism; in reality, racism was a symptom of the original sin of greed. The *Anti-Greed Gospel* dismantles deficient definitions of racism and reminds us that greed is what generates, animates, and sustains racial prejudice—both past and present. This book, properly understood and applied, has the potential to topple our monuments to Mammon and make room for real racial justice in both church and society."

—**Jemar Tisby,** *New York Times* bestselling author of *The Color of Compromise* and *The Spirit of Justice*; professor, Simmons College of Kentucky

"The love of money is the root of all kinds of evil, including racism. Malcolm Foley is a thinker who makes you think. In his debut work, Foley unpacks the theological and sociological layers of racism. He rightly identifies the center of American racism, which is greed—greed that costs human lives. Foley's book builds a strong case for what's really fueling the lie of race and the horrors of racism, but he doesn't leave us hopeless. This book offers us a necessary antidote to racism if we put down the delusions and temptations of greed."

—**Christina Edmondson,** coauthor of *Faithful Antiracism* and *Truth's Table*

"Malcolm Foley continues the radical tradition by showing us how greed produces racism. He calls us away from anti-racist virtue signaling and brings us to the feet of Jesus, where we can either beg God's mercy for our racist greed or justify ourselves into condemnation. He reminds us that the church's fight against anti-Black lynching and its struggle for economic justice and solidarity are the same fight."

—**Jonathan Tran**, associate professor, Baylor University; author of *Asian Americans and the Spirit of Racial Capitalism*

"*The Anti-Greed Gospel* is both seriously convicting and saturated with hope—real hope that is both disruptive and full of wonder. I learned. I lamented. I leapt. Malcolm Foley points us to the alternative society that the church has always been, calling us to economic solidarity, creative anti-violence, and prophetic truth telling. In this, we are a people that isn't striving to redeem the world but rather revealing that the world has already been changed by the life, death, and resurrection of Jesus Christ. May churches read this book together and practice living in the reality of the kingdom and the love for our Lord and for our neighbor."

—**Aimee Byrd**, author of *Saving Face* and *The Hope in Our Scars*

THE
ANTI-GREED
GOSPEL

THE ANTI-GREED GOSPEL

Why the Love of Money Is the Root of Racism *and* How the Church Can Create a New Way Forward

Malcolm Foley

Brazos Press

a division of Baker Publishing Group
Grand Rapids, Michigan

Published by Brazos Press
a division of Baker Publishing Group
Grand Rapids, Michigan
BrazosPress.com

Printed in the United States of America

Library of Congress Cataloging-in-Publication Data
Names: Foley, Malcolm, 1990– author
Title: The anti-greed gospel : why the love of money is the root of racism and how the church can create a new way forward / Malcolm Foley.
Description: Grand Rapids, Michigan : Brazos Press, a division of Baker Publishing Group, [2025] | Includes bibliographical references.
Identifiers: LCCN 2024029232 | ISBN 9781493447909 ebook | ISBN 9781587436529 casebound | ISBN 9781587436307 paperback
Subjects: LCSH: Economics—Religious aspects—Christianity
Classification: LCC BR115.E3 F5668 2025 | DDC 261.8/5—dc23/eng/20240827
LC record available at https://lccn.loc.gov/2024029232

Cover design by Darren Welch Design

Baker Publishing Group publications use paper produced from sustainable forestry practices and postconsumer waste whenever possible.

25 26 27 28 29 30 31   7 6 5 4 3 2 1

To the two great brides:

my wife, Desiree,
and the bride of Christ,
the church militant

Perhaps one of you will say, "Every day, you talk about covetousness." Would that I could speak about it every night too; would that I could do so, following you about in the market-place, and at your table; would that both wives, and friends, and children, and domestics, and tillers of the soil, and neighbors, and the very pavement and walls, could ever shout forth this word. . . . For this malady hath seized upon all the world, and occupies the souls of all, and great is the tyranny of Mammon.

—John Chrysostom, *Homilies on the Gospel of St. John*

Contents

Acknowledgments

I t is a dream come true to complete my first book, and it is a dream that has required the help of many to reach fruition. I think of David Whitacre, the comparative religion teacher I had in high school who birthed in me a love for church history and theology. I think of my mom and dad, who have always modeled the faith for me. I think of my mentors and close friends, Jon and Anita Hinkson, who remain two of the most Christlike individuals I have ever had the pleasure to know. Also, I want to thank those who read and commented on the drafts, especially Tom Millay, Jonathan Tran, and Tyler Davis. These are a few of the individuals who have made me the person I am today.

Others, however, have significantly shaped my thought. This book would look quite a bit different if it had been written three years ago. But in February 2022, I reread Martin Luther King Jr. and encountered Antonio González and Jonathan Tran. The pieces began to come together, pieces that had been floating in my mind for years. The book that you hold in your hands is the result of that coalescence.

I want to thank my family: my wife, Desiree, and my daughters, Jasmyne Ida and Junia, both of whom slowed my writing down, as children typically do. But they have also made it richer, as they remind me on a daily basis why I do the work I do. It is my hope that this book contributes to a better world for them.

Last, I must shout out to my church, Mosaic Waco. They have graciously endured my preaching and my constant calls for them to "gird their loins." This book is the fruit of my service to that congregation, and I look forward to many more years, Lord willing, of building the kind of community to which this book bears witness.

Introduction

Breaking the Cycle

Ten years ago, if you had told me that I would one day write a book on racism, I would have laughed at you. Sure, I wanted to write and contribute to scholarly conversations—but not about race. I had no desire to be another Black man pigeonholed into being a race scholar. But the Lord had other plans. And a particularly powerful woman served as his instrument to make me reconsider what path I would pursue: Ida B. Wells (1862–1931).

In 1892, Wells wrote one of the most significant works of myth-busting in the lynching era with the publication of her editorial pamphlet *Southern Horrors*. In contrast to the popular understanding that the brutal lynchings of Black Americans were acts of communal justice meted out against criminals, Wells framed lynching as a violent arm of white supremacy. In *Southern Horrors*, she also noted both the reason for lynching and the best way to stop it. After noting that Black people were the economic backbone of the South, she suggested that Black laborers withdraw en masse from the South to resist lynching.

Why? Because "the white man's dollar is his god. . . . The appeal to the white man's pocket has ever been more effectual than all the appeals ever made to his conscience."[1]

If ever a quote could so briefly sum up the history of race and racism, it would be that one.

Race is not primarily about hate and ignorance. It's about greed. It always has been. And the purpose of this book is that you might understand the unholy relationship between race and greed, best understood not as a marriage but in terms of parentage: race and racism are children of Mammon.

Why say "Mammon" instead of "money" or "riches"? And why capitalize it? Very simply, when we discuss racism and mobilize people against it, we must remember the high stakes of what we're doing: we are talking about idolatry. *Pleonexia*, the Greek word variably translated as "covetousness" or "greed" in the New Testament, is the evil at root: the constant desire for more, the drive to accumulate. This desire was the impetus for the construction of race, and it continues to feed it. Our response to greed must be relentless. In the apostle's terms, we must put it to death, because greed is idolatry (see Col. 3:5). If this is true, then greed is a breaking of, at minimum, the first and tenth commandments: that we are to have no other gods before the Lord and that we are not to covet.

But we can go further. By the end of this introduction, you will see that the making of race and racism is linked to the breaking of *seven* of the Ten Commandments. If that's true, as I believe it is, then we have quite the task ahead of us. The stakes are cosmic: we are engaged in a battle of gods, and this book is precipitated by the fact that rival gods require blood sacrifice. Mammon is no different. Jesus is not exaggerating when he says we cannot serve two masters: God and Mammon. The parallelism ought not be ignored. We have a choice; there is no both/and option. We will hate one and love the other. But the fact of the matter is that Mammon will demand our blood, the blood of our brothers and sisters, and the blood of our neighbors. Our accumulation necessitates exploitation. And the exploitation that upholds our current economy of racialized capitalism requires murder. These claims sound extreme, but the history of race supports them and has often put the sword in the hands of people who have claimed to be followers of Christ. Race was and is a child of Mammon, and the powers and principalities would like us to join Mammon's family. It must not be so. We are to be children of God. Our gospel is inextricably an anti-greed gospel.

For some of you, talking about race in terms of greed rather than hate may seem like old hat. For others, it may be new. Don't worry; I was once where you are. But after my eyes were opened, I could not return to the way I was. My hope is that after reading this book, the same will be true of you.

Why Me?

I'd like to take a bit more space to walk you briefly through my transformation before getting explicit about the powers and principalities that we face and how we can best resist them, personally and communally.

Up until my undergraduate years, I was a math, natural science, and computer science student, poised to follow my peers into either engineering or the sciences. In high school, however, I took a comparative religion class where my atheistic teacher challenged my faith in a way that it had not been challenged before—something for which I am deeply grateful. My love for the history of Christianity was born. When I got to college to study religion, my father encouraged me to use my love for math in a way that was more marketable, so I chose finance as a second major. After college, as academia began to draw me in, the questions that face every scholar loomed over me: What will I study? There was precious little overlap between the history of Christianity and finance. What was I to do?

I decided to focus on the Greek church fathers. I was enamored with the Egyptian patriarch Cyril of Alexandria and the seventh-century monk Maximus the Confessor. Their accounts of Christ were cosmic, drawing me into an all-encompassing understanding of Christ's work in me, the body of Christ, and the world. I thought I would dive deeply into these figures, perhaps linking them to another prominent Christian theologian, John Calvin. Yet the Lord would not let it be so. While studying for my PhD, discouraged by the glut of Calvin scholarship, I decided to transition to the Puritans, expertly dodging a voice that called me to consider the history of race in America. I shut that voice out for fear of being pigeonholed. Yet it did not get quieter. My work on the Reformation, the Puritans, and the Greek fathers, though fruitful, was my Jonah-like fleeing to Tarshish. Racial violence was my Nineveh.

During a class on post–Civil War Christianity, my professor, fellow students, and I discussed the fundamentalist-modernist controversy, in which early twentieth-century white Christians battled for power in seminaries, biblical interpretation, and other fields of study. This one-sentence summary might offend some of my fellow historians, but it captures my internal reaction to those conversations as I considered a glaring omission: What about the thousands of Black men being killed by mobs at the time of the fundamentalist-modernist controversy? I knew this era as the lynching era. It was a period when, under the auspices of "popular justice," white mobs killed Black men and women brutally and publicly, hanging them, shooting them to pieces, burning them alive, and visiting on Black communities a seemingly indiscriminate wave of terror. What were Black Christians doing at this point in time? How does one survive and thrive in a society poised and organized for one's death? Finding few scholarly resources to answer these questions, I focused my PhD dissertation on them; you will find some of the fruit of my research in this book.[2]

After finishing my doctorate, however, my questions deepened. The year 2020 came and went with perhaps the largest mobilization of people in protest since the civil rights movement (1954–68) and the Vietnam War (1955–75). Police brutality was in the news constantly. Videos of public murder circulated on social media. People, especially my white brothers and sisters, were reading book after book about racial justice. It appeared that eyes were being opened. Reconciliation was back in full force as the answer; animosity and ignorance had taken root, we were told in Christian circles. Education and relationships would be the most reliable ways forward, but they would not be enough. We were reminded that systems were at play as well, necessarily widening our purview. People who had never used the word *systemic* to describe racism suddenly figured out what that meant, which was that racism extended beyond individual hearts and minds.

Many who experienced this progression didn't know that it mirrored the progression of the 1960s as well: the time when many took the term *racist* as an epithet synonymous with *hater*. Many were probably also unaware that we had done all of this before. Even during the civil rights movement, people who were exposed to the brutality of Jim Crow saw integration as the answer—rather than economically and politically restructuring the whole of American society, as Martin Luther King Jr. would argue in favor of in 1967.[3] It was easier to view justice as the presence of nice multicolored faces rather than something requiring material sacrifice and solidarity.

As Christians reckoned with the violence around them, King's speech at the March on Washington was rearticulated as the Christian ideal of racial reconciliation. But something was missing. What exactly?

The answer to that question lies in the full title of the march at which King articulated his dream, which he saw turn into a nightmare. In fact, the optimism of that speech was, for King, tempered by his growing understanding that America was deeply captive to Mammon. The march's full title is the March on Washington for Jobs and Freedom. King never conceived of racial justice apart from economic justice.

That fact has not changed, though our appetite for it has diminished. One of the purposes of this book is to reinvigorate our appetite and to remind us that love and justice are fundamentally material realities that require redistribution and solidarity.

The importance of this rather simple connection pressed me deeper into the pursuit of racial justice. And it provided the impetus and the foundation for the book you hold in your hands. At its center is the claim that hate and ignorance are not at the root of race; rather, that root is greed. Notably, King, especially in the last few years of his life, drew attention to the three-headed evil that has plagued Western civilization: racism, materialism, and militarism. More pointedly, however, he drew attention to them in their most violent and common instantiations: white supremacy, capitalism, and war.

These have been the inextricable evils of our day; we cannot address one of them apart from the two others. After revisiting King's framework, I realized that *self-interest* binds these three evils together. This led me to recognize the three evils for what they really are: a demonic feedback loop of self-interest. This loop has three elements, as we will see in chapter 1: we use others for personal gain, we violently protect that gain when others protest, and we create ideas to justify our exploitation of one another and our violence. Put differently, the cycle begins with political and economic exploitation, continues by violently enforcing that exploitation, and is justified by the concept of race. This cycle explains why racism is both brutal and resilient: it is not fueled primarily by hatred but rather by material desires on our part and the spiritual power of those

Paul calls "principalities" (Eph. 6:12 KJV). No wonder lasting peace is so far from reality.

This foundation in material desires provides the basis for this book: If racism is chiefly about greed rather than hate, what does that mean for our communities? This work focuses on the second arm of the cycle, which is violent enforcement that continually reaches back to exploit and repeatedly reaches forward for justification. Lynching is this enforcement's historical springboard—that most disturbing element of American history we would like to think is far behind us. Yet if we recognize the roots of both that practice and racialized violence today, we can better invest in our health and life together.

But a focus on the violent effects of greed reveals something else that ought to inform how we articulate the gospel: that we, particularly in the United States, believe we can ignore Christ's declaration. We have tried for a long time to serve both God and Mammon, and millions have died as a result. What remains for us is to understand this history and to live in light of it. Thus, a reckoning with history requires robust theological and ethical work as well.

The Anti-Greed Gospel is just such a work of history, theology, and ethics. The history of racialized violence will (and ought to) sicken you. With this history is another history, that of economic exploitation as the root from which racism springs forth. Greed is racism's fuel. Only when this history is understood can the proper theological and ethical interventions take place. Historically, racialized capitalism, wielding racial violence like a sword, has killed in two ways: it has taken human life, and it has blurred and distorted theological and ethical reasoning. In this book, I draw attention to role models who attempted to resist both of these death-dealing impulses. But the book's primary thrust is to imagine how we can build Christian communities that resist the death-dealing talons and tendrils of racialized capitalism. Such a project begins with this acknowledgment: *an anti-racist community is an anti-greed community*. An anti-racist community is a community in which the desire for more is excised and replaced with a robust embrace of the communion of the saints. Such a community follows the logic of the kingdom of God: authority and resources are to be shared rather than hoarded.

Only when our communities share rather than hoard will we be able to show the world what Jesus expresses as the ideal to his disciples in John 13: the world will know that we are his disciples by our love. Such love is not simply an emotion or even merely a series of actions. Love is also a political economy and a way of life that undermines the kingdoms of the world. By *political economy*, I mean a social arrangement with a particular account of power and resources and how they should be distributed. I invite you to walk with me on this thorny road. My prayer is that we come out on the other side of the journey as brothers and sisters deeply devoted to the love of God and a deep care for the material and spiritual needs of our neighbors.

A New Definition of Terms

Before continuing with the particulars of the history of lynching, it is important for me to define the terms you will see repeatedly in this book. I should begin with this thought: race is about money, and the kingdom is about Jesus. This statement is both polemical and definitional; what I'm saying is as important as what I'm arguing against.

The polemical import of the above-mentioned beginning thought is this: race and racism are not fundamentally about hate or ignorance; they are creations of greed. Sociologist Oliver Cromwell Cox phrases it this way: "This, then, is the beginning of modern race relations. It was not an abstract, natural, immemorial feeling of mutual antipathy between groups, but rather a practical exploitative relationship with its socio-attitudinal facilitation."[4] If this is true, then one of the most relevant anti-racist verses can be found in the Sermon on the Mount: "No one can serve two masters; for you will hate the one and love the other, or you will be devoted to the one and despise the other. You cannot serve both God and money" (Matt. 6:24). In making this claim, I do not mean that we can reduce everything deemed "racial" down to money. Rather, I mean that race has historically worked in such a way as to entangle the exploited and the exploiter alike, to the point that we no longer recognize the snare. Yet Cox again bracingly reminds us, as he paraphrases Adam Smith, that "they who teach and finance race prejudice are by no means such fools as the majority of those who believe and practice it."[5] If we as Christians are to avoid one thing, it must be foolishness.

In saying these things, I repeat an insight I take most immediately from theologian Jonathan Tran and the broader Black radical tradition; political economy, the historical-material context that perpetuates racist thinking and racist social conditions, brings us closer to an understanding of what race does, how it harms, and how we can be agents of liberation.[6] Political economy may not explain everything that race does or is, but it explains enough of it to mobilize us to love our neighbors robustly. It also focuses us on shaping lives of repentance, particularly with respect to the sin historically at the root of racism: greed.

Thinking in these terms requires a shift in mindset for many of us. In Christian circles, especially evangelical ones, we are quick to turn to relationships as the primary tool for racial justice. For some, the problem is hate: if we learn to love one another, racism will fade. For others, the problem is ignorance: if we just know each other and our histories better, we will be able to heal the wounds rent open by white supremacy. This approach, however, covers only the surface level of the egregiously public acts of racism that we hear about, witness, and experience. I'm not satisfied with the fact that the Klan is somewhat embarrassed to march openly (though in recent years, they have seemed to be less embarrassed). I want to contribute to a society that makes such a group ridiculous, unattractive, and irrelevant. The evil stoked by the Klan and other such groups should be starved with love rather than fed by outrage. In order to overcome racism, however, it must be addressed at its root rather than at its fruit.

Focusing on money or political economy in one's treatment of race is not new, but it has fallen out of popular memory. Consider one of the most popular definitions of *racism*, which is "prejudice plus power." Such a definition sounds reasonable. It mixes the personal and the institutional, the two elements we are constantly encouraged to keep in mind. Solutions vary: Perhaps we are to give power to the powerless. Perhaps we are to revise our views of one another. Perhaps we are to combine the two. These suggestions sound reasonable. But they dilute the nature of the problems we face. Race has been invoked for more than five hundred years not merely as a basis for hatred but as a reason for death. The stakes extend beyond an individual you know (or don't know) treating you with ill will or shaping your material circumstances.

The United States has formed and mobilized structures of exploitation that disproportionately disadvantage and kill certain people, particularly those racialized as Black, Indigenous, Asian, and Latino/a. But this is not just a national story. To expand from the personal to the institutional and the national is like making the move that Paul makes in Ephesians 6, where he argues that the battle is not with flesh and blood but rather with the rulers, the authorities, the powers of this dark world, the spiritual forces of evil. This is true, but it is not yet comprehensive. Racial narratives and their murdering talons and tendrils are global. Their reach, however, is not primarily the reach of ideas but the reach of money. Racism properly and broadly understood is like the head of a mythical Hydra—a bestial manifestation of cosmic and apocalyptic evil.

That description seems catastrophic. It is. It might also appear unassailable. But it is not. You will read about profound human and supernatural evil in the chapters that follow. But more importantly, in these pages you will encounter the Light who vanquishes evil. Christ, by his death and resurrection, has actually defeated the powers and has also gathered a people—a people called to be an alternative political, spiritual, and economic community in this world. After all, I do not only want us to remember that race is primarily about money; I also want us to remember that the kingdom of God is about Jesus. I am reminded by Latin American theologians how much the Gospels and Jesus's preaching focus on the kingdom, an ordering of affairs at odds with the kingdoms of this world. Right now, the kingdoms of the world are governed by the political logic of domination and the economic logic of exploitation. *Power* is often defined as the ability to tell people what to do and the fact that they do what you say. For Jesus and his people, power is only rightly mobilized as self-sacrificial love.

We must remember that the temptations to exploit and dominate one another and to justify such domination come from a common root—namely, self-interest. James, the brother of Jesus, says it concisely: "What causes fights and quarrels among you? Don't they come from your desires that battle within you? You desire but do not have, so you kill. You covet but you cannot get what you want, so you quarrel and fight" (James 4:1–2). If we question what racism does rather than what racism is, our history reminds us that its most fundamental purpose is to establish systems of wealth and advantage that beneficiaries, regardless of race, seek to perpetuate without being trampled on by those same systems. For many of us, our first thought when we consider a system of which we are a part is "How can I make it to the top?" rather than "How does this fare for those at the bottom?"

I, along with the apostle Paul, am convinced that human evil is not the only evil that the Christian has to struggle against. To be sure, humans do profoundly evil things, but I also know that they do so with supernatural assistance. When one considers the longevity and brutality of racial violence, as well as the consistent efforts to hide or ignore it, one would be hard pressed to chalk it all up to human ingenuity. The powers and principalities are at work in this history. Grappling with this fact also reminds us that our enemies are not one another; rather, our enemies are those who seek to enslave us all: sin, death, and the devil.

What's So Bad about Racism?

Before we go further, we have another question to address: What precisely is so bad about racism? Part of me hopes that I ask this question to a sympathetic audience who knows that something is wrong with how we view race. But perhaps you can't quite put your finger on what is so diabolical about the construct. Your first thoughts might be that it is unfair, that it leads to prejudging others without knowing them, that it breaks people apart, that it precipitates violence, and that when you really interrogate it, it's just a made-up concept. All these thoughts are generally true, and their corresponding realities are bad, but they are disparate. They can be summarized, as so many things can be, by a threefold recognition: that race and racism *lie*, *kill*, and *steal*, not unlike the thief Jesus speaks of in John 10. That is, race and acts of racism are enemies of truth, enemies of life, and enemies of material equality and flourishing. In these three sins, however, we also find that, at the very least, seven of the Ten Commandments are implicated, and this ought to blow our minds. But the effect should not stop there. By seeing the extent of the evil, we also ought to steel ourselves for battle against the powers and principalities that seek to bring us into subjection. That work begins with addressing lies.

The Lies of Race and Racism

The lies of race and racism take multiple forms. The lie of superiority and inferiority is the easiest for the Christian to dispel, at least in theory. Racist ideas, especially as we commonly think of them, encourage us to believe that members of a particular racial group (most often but not exclusively Blacks) are inferior to members of another racial group (most often but not exclusively whites). While this is not the most dangerous element of race and racism, it is the one most Christians like to focus on, perhaps because it appears to us to be the easiest to address. Particularly in evangelical circles, it is common to respond to issues of race and racism by referring to Ephesians 2. Christ has broken down the walls of separation, we are told. Just as Christ's redemption brought together Jew and gentile, so it also reaches across the lines of race.

Christ has done such things. Christ's redemption is that powerful. But those truths do not tell us anything about how race actually functions in society—that is, they tell us little about what race has *done* or continues to *do*. If racism were only about lies, then truth telling would be adequate. Yet no amount of truth telling will close the economic gaps that still seem to give race meaning. Nor will truth telling stop the police officer's bullet from piercing the disabled Black person's body. Nor will truth telling alone remove the shackles from the unjustly incarcerated.

It is, however, very important that we address and recognize lies as lies. If we assume or argue that a causal relationship exists between the made-up category of race and anything about a person besides the way they are treated, we reveal ourselves to be subject to lies. According to the brilliant work of Adolph Reed Jr., race is "a taxonomy of ascriptive difference, that is, an ideology that constructs populations as groups and sorts them into hierarchies of capacity, civic worth, and desert based on 'natural' or essential characteristics attributed to them."[7] Said another way, race is a series of lies: the hierarchies of capacity are untrue, the hierarchies of civic worth are untrue, and the hierarchies of desert are untrue. Still, despite its untruths, race remains persuasive and powerful.

For the Christian, race as a construct violates the ninth commandment: "You shall not give false testimony against your neighbor" (Exod. 20:16). The Westminster Larger Catechism reminds us that the Ten Commandments bear within them both prohibitions *and* duties. The catechism teaches us not only not to lie about one another but also to love one another by rejoicing in others' good reputation, by promoting and rejoicing in the truth, and by distancing ourselves from and discouraging lies, slander, and injustice. Race as a construct, however, creates and justifies difference, gives credence to unjust states of affairs, and encourages suffering people to swallow their pain rather than seek liberation.

Truth is important and will set us free. But it is insufficient. And that is because those who seek to construct race and mobilize racism do more than just lie to us. They kill and steal from us too.

The Resulting Death

The lies are bad. But the resulting death is worse. Because I am covering the lynching of Afro-Americans in this book, I will emphasize Afro-American deaths. But racism's death toll extends beyond the Afro-American community. Lynching regimes also targeted Chinese and Mexican workers (their identity as workers will be made especially relevant in our discussion of the next evil). Consider those who died in the forced marches from their homes to the coast of Western Africa. Consider the millions who died of dysentery, scurvy, and suicide in the Middle Passage. Consider that the soon-to-be-enslaved would suffer from malnutrition and lie in their own fecal matter for days. Consider that after the ordeal at sea they would be subjected to the chattel slavery that could then lead to their death in the Americas. Consider those who died by suicide in the "seasoning" process of slavery, in which they were submitted to sexual assault, familial separation, and excruciating labor.[8]

Slavery, however, justified the creation of race as we think of it rather than resulted from it. So perhaps you may think it unfair to lay those deaths at the feet of racism. Let us turn, then, to the postbellum period. Immediately following the Civil War (1861–65), the United States witnessed the rise of white paramilitary groups like the Ku Klux Klan and the White League. According to the law, particularly the Reconstruction Amendments, newly freed men and women were full citizens. According to white supremacist groups, however, newly freed people were political and economic obstacles. These supremacists did not merely frighten; they also killed.

But the most publicly violent instantiation of white supremacy was yet to come. From 1883 to 1941, more than three thousand Black men were lynched by mobs in the United States, and women and children were not spared from this violence.[9] That number may seem small in the grand scheme, but lynching's brutality and publicity were largely unprecedented. As an example, in 1918, Hampton Smith, a plantation owner in Brooks County, Georgia, was shot and killed by one of his Black workers, a man named Sydney Johnson. Smith was known for abusing his workers, a reputation that made hiring difficult. So Smith took advantage of an oppressive system: debt peonage, also known as convict leasing. What that means is that he would bail offenders out of jail, people who had typically been arrested for petty offenses, and have them work off their debt. Johnson, nineteen, had been arrested for "rolling dice" and fined thirty dollars; he was one such unfortunate person.

After Smith refused to pay him his earned wages and beat him, Johnson shot and killed his employer. This sparked a manhunt for Johnson and those assumed to be coconspirators. At least eleven people were killed. One was a woman named Mary Turner.

Turner had publicly objected to the murder of her husband by the mob hunting Johnson. She also threatened to swear out warrants for those responsible. An area paper called those remarks "unwise," and the mob turned on her. So she ran, only to be caught and taken to a place called Folsom's Bridge, on the Brooks and Lowndes Counties' shared border. The mob tied her by her ankles, hung her upside down from a tree, covered her in gasoline and oil, and set her ablaze. She was also eight months pregnant at the time, and the mob, according to an investigator's account, cut the baby out of her while she was still alive and stomped the baby to death. Then, after Turner was dead, the mob fired hundreds of bullets into her body.

This brutality is sickening and, for many, unexplainable. What could drive a mob to such extreme violence, particularly against a woman and an unborn baby? As complex as we might think it is, the answer is rather simple: hate. Material, burning hate. There were, of course, justifying narratives that pervaded the lynching era, narratives we will discuss in the following chapter. But these stories were smoke screens for a deep and abiding hatred: a refusal to see other human beings as human beings to be loved, supported, and cared for. This deeper impulse is the enemy that must be excised from our communities.

We know that murder breaks the sixth commandment, but it is important that we understand precisely why. The Westminster Catechism helps us here too. It is not enough for us not to kill our neighbor; we're commanded to love one another. Love is fundamentally active. The end result of the construction of race and the mobilization of racism is love's opposite: murder. Theologian Herman Bavinck frames the failure to love as "*heartlessness*—a loss of natural affection, lovelessness; the lack of all compassion and mercy; harshness; viewing the stranger as an enemy, as a barbarian, as someone of a lower order, of different descent."[10] This is what we see when we witness racial violence: the natural affection that we owe our fellow human beings is suppressed and clouded by false narratives of racial difference. The result is not merely that we live out lies. It is that we actively contribute to death.

One more sin is at hand when we consider race and racism, and it's the most pervasive and insidious one. This is the one that takes up most of our time in this book. I say the most insidious because it is the sin that we are conditioned to both ignore and justify. It is also a sin the Jesus warns against on many occasions. That sin is, of course, greed.

The Theft

Greed, rather simply, is when desire outstrips need. When I am driven to accumulate for myself beyond what I need, I fall victim to greed. Greed has prompted the construction of race and racism. In addition to the commandments broken by killing and lying, the greed that precipitated the creation of race breaks five more of the Ten Commandments.

A short pamphlet from the American Anti-Slavery Society in the mid-nineteenth century made the compelling argument that slavery facilitates the breaking of all ten of the commandments. I want to take the issue to another level: not merely to say that race *facilitates* the breaking of these commandments, but to say that it fundamentally *depends on* the breaking of the commandments. If this is true, then obeying the commandments will help to break race and racism. Remove the foundation and the house falls. For example, adultery and the dishonoring of parents can be by-products of a racist society, as the history of sexual exploitation and abuse and family separation coincides with the history of racism in many heartbreaking ways. The breaking of the Sabbath and the dishonoring of the Lord's Day are continually encouraged by a political economy that requires profit for survival. After all, why would you choose not to work one day a week when you can make money, whether that money depends on exploitation or not? But the commandments against adultery, dishonoring of parents, and dishonoring the Sabbath are the three commandments *incidentally* broken by the construction of race, not *fundamentally* broken by it. The remaining commandments are fundamental to the particular type of greed that has made race so compelling in American history. If that is true, then resisting greed will also help us obey the Lord more comprehensively!

The first and second commandments are broken by devotion to Mammon. Mammon is both a god to obey and a graven image to which many bow. Mammon is irrevocably material, but it is not content with your body. It must also have your soul. The pursuit of profit compelled slave traders to pack human beings, like so many pieces of luggage, into the hulls of ships for the sake of "efficiency." The pursuit of profit facilitated the worker abuse that Hampton Smith perpetrated, setting in motion events that led to Mary Turner and her baby's murders. Ultimately, an insatiable and bloodthirsty god demanded these actions.

The most heartbreaking and commandment-breaking aspect of race is how it has compelled many to take the name of the Lord in vain, thus breaking the third commandment. Taking the Lord's name in vain is not just about haphazardly verbally referring to God. It is about associating the name of God with evil, emptying the name of God of its beauty and holiness. The construction of race required many Christians to insist that God willed slavery. Pastors, out of one side of their mouth, affirmed that Africans were created in the image of God and then, out of the other side, spoke of how "emancipat[ing] our negroes" would be tantamount to acting against God's providence.[11] James Henley Thornwell, a prominent proslavery thinker in American history, was one such example. Thornwell justified slavery, as many others did at the time, with varying levels of honesty about its brutality and an obvious affirmation of white superiority. Thornwell was particularly dangerous because he taught the ontological equality of white Americans and Black Africans yet also justified the latter's material subjugation. This contradiction showed up in many theologians' arguments, as well as in the American legal system. For example, in 1667 Virginia enacted a law stating that baptism didn't free slaves from bondage, reminding them that while they may be free in the Lord, they were not free from their human masters. This disjunction of the spiritual and the material, paired with saying that this disjunction is God's will rather than the manifestation of one's greed, is a paradigmatic example of taking the Lord's name in vain.

Of course, more can be said. The eighth and tenth commandments direct us to avoid both the natural outcome of greed (i.e., theft) and its root (i.e., covetousness). In fact, this outcome and root are mutually defining and mutually reinforcing: covetousness is greed, which is theft. All three feed and finance race and racism. We often categorize one another in order to take advantage of those who fall outside of the boundaries drawn, and that advantage is, more often than not, financial. Race and racism were created because some people wanted more resources, wanted them cheaply, and were willing to do whatever it took to accumulate those resources. This is the history that we will narrate in the coming chapter, but it is also the key to unlocking the decisions that we see in our neighborhoods: decisions about where and how to build housing, how property taxes are determined and paid, where to build highways, what schools to invest in, and countless other decisions.

You may think that the equation of greed, covetousness, and theft is sloppy. But for our purposes, especially when we imagine becoming a truly anti-racist Christian community, these three phenomena are synonymous. Two of the Great Doctors of the Eastern Church, Basil the Great and John Chrysostom, are the best resources for the body of Christ on this point: greed does not merely lead to theft. Greed *is* theft.

We will spend more time with Basil and Chrysostom at the end of the book, but for now a few points will suffice. Basil, preaching on the conversation between Jesus and the rich young ruler, views the young man's sin as greed, understood as a failure to love his neighbor as himself. Affirming that "care for the needy requires the expenditure of wealth," Basil utters a heart-stopping line in his sermon, aptly titled *To the Rich*: "The more you abound in wealth, the more you lack in love."[12] Basil, in his particular context, sees that the Scriptures frame a world in which accumulation almost always happens at someone else's expense, and that person is often needy. Thus, the more you have and hold, the less you love your neighbor.

Basil here gives the reason for Christian generosity: it is not an extra nice-to-have element of the Christian life; rather, it is a fundamental act of obedience to the Great Commandments and, particularly, to the eighth and tenth commandments. It is difficult to steal and covet when your primary relationship with goods is thinking of how they can be redistributed to meet needs. None of this denies familial obligation, but it does remind us that love of neighbor requires redistribution, not just a different attitude about money.

Chrysostom similarly calls us to lives of simplicity rather than luxury, specifically so that we have enough to give. In fact, Chrysostom, like Basil, marshals the Scriptures to show that "not only the theft of others' goods but also the failure to share one's own goods with others is theft and swindle and defraudation."[13] The only reason God allows us to have more,

Chrysostom argues, is so that we will distribute our surplus to those in need. The story of race, however, is a narrative that allows people to accumulate more in order to increase their power and influence, not for the sake of the common good but for the sake of selfish ambition.

Thus, *seven* of the Ten Commandments (the first, second, third, sixth, eighth, ninth, and tenth) are substantively implicated in the creation of race as a category and the mobilization of racism as an evil. Greed, murder, and lies pervade race and racism and are inextricable from them. Because each of these realities is inimical to the gospel of Jesus Christ, the church—those who claim to be citizens of the kingdom of God—must resist them in all their forms. This book aims to show you examples of how that has gone right or wrong, and it aims to give you some ways to shape truly anti-racist communities. In fact, the goal is not that your community would be anti-racist or even anti-greed per se, as inextricable as those realities are. The goal is that our communities would be truly worthy of the name "Christian."

PART 1

OUR HISTORY OF GREED, RACE, AND RACIAL CAPITALISM

1

How Greed
Gave Birth to Race

What is [racism]? It is the phenomenon of the capitalist exploitation of peoples and its complementary social
attitude.

—Oliver Cox, *Caste, Class, and Race*

L et's start with a simple question: Where did our global
economy come from? Capitalism requires capital, resources that can be used to produce the goods that we
enjoy. The readiest example of such capital is land.

In the late fifteenth century, this particular resource began to
change hands in wide swaths. It was the colonial era, when Europeans explored the world, saw that it was good, and reached
out to grab it. Did any part of our global economy originate
without covetousness and theft? American history depends on
these realities, and to a certain extent, world history from the
sixteenth century onward has depended on them.

That theft was specific: theft *from* particular people and theft
of people. The transatlantic slave trade enabled Europe and

the United States to become the powerhouses they are today. Europeans could move goods from and to Asia, Africa, and the Americas. Their competitive advantage was their might: their ships and their cannons. Historian Walter Rodney sums up the result of this arrangement well: "What was called international trade was nothing but the extension overseas of European interests."[1] Portugal was the nation most responsible for its beginning.

When the Portuguese began the European wing of the African slave trade, they did so because it was profitable, not because they were racist. There were markets to coordinate and expand, specifically for cotton, spices, and silks. The Portuguese and the Spanish would buy cotton cloth from India, which they would take to Africa to trade for slaves, who would be used in the Americas to mine gold, which would be used to buy more goods from India. This cycle encapsulates how these nations grew their wealth. But this economic state of affairs depended on colonization, exploitation, and violence. What allowed Europeans to mine gold and silver in the Americas? It was not that they asked nicely. Colonial violence and attempted genocide spurred European wealth building. To bring it home to us in the United States, one author summarizes the problem this way: "The massive theft that was slavery is the tainted wellspring of American capitalism. In the United States, capital—accrued for the wealthiest over generations—was built on the lacerated backs of Black people."[2]

Before we go further, we need to define both *capitalism* and *race*. And if you're concerned that I've mentioned capitalism and will be outlining a number of its evils, please know that I am not proposing a state-run economy. Capitalism is the water in which we swim. Because we are aware of the failures and often brutality of the alternative economic arrangement (i.e., centralized planning), it is easy to think in terms of binaries. I hope we can be more creative than that. But for this work to continue and for us to battle the powers and principalities, we have to name our economic systems. Even if capitalism is the devil we know (or at least *think* we know), we must not be deceived about its devilish qualities. As long as such an economy depends on the oppression and subjugation of image bearers, it is tainted.

The short definitions that follow will help us to understand the demonic cycle of self-interest, and because capitalism is chronologically first, we will address it first.

Capitalism Defined

Capitalism can be understood as the combination of three necessary factors: private ownership of the means of production, wage labor, and market exchange—that is, the resources needed to produce goods (land, machinery, materials, etc.) lie in private hands, people work for wages, and the goods created by employees are exchanged. Two types of people exist in this arrangement: the capitalist class, which owns the means of production, and workers, who labor for them. Nothing, at face value, is inherently wrong with any of this.

But we have to dig deeper. What kind of wages is best in this system? What drives these markets? Economist and philosopher Adam Smith tells us a practical but lamentable truth: we as human beings need each other, but it is almost useless to expect aid from others based on their benevolence. So what do we often do? We show others how what benefits us also benefits them.[3] This tactic can be observed in many of our personal interactions. When I go to a restaurant, what's more important to the restaurant is that I can pay money, not that I'm hungry. As R & B singer Barrett Strong says, "Your love gives me such a thrill, but your love don't pay my bills."[4] Once the bill comes, the waiter will not accept my satiated hunger as payment.

Modern capitalism, as we know it, is guided, inspired, and maintained by self-interest. But self-interest is not a sustainable base. In fact, it is a dangerous one. The assumption is that self-interest and greed are interchangeable: I assume that my neighbor wants to make more money, that my neighbor wants to accumulate. So especially if I am a worker at my neighbor's mercy, I try to narrate my need in a way that matches their desire. "I need a job" is unfortunately not a compelling answer to a job recruiter asking you why they should hire you, even though it is most often the truest answer. Most employers do not feel obliged to give just anyone a job; rather, they are encouraged to do so if applicants can submit their self-interest to the interest of the corporation. The role of wages is at play: you are compensated to spend your time in the best interest of those you work for. The questions that I asked above, about wages and what drives the market, are answered in favor of the owners because they wield the most power in the system. Your material need is not what pushes the economy forward, nor is it what drives economic progress. Your need matters only insofar as it supports an additional factor in a capitalistic system.

That additional factor in modern capitalism is profit maximization. In order to flourish as a business, you have to grow. Your profits can't remain stagnant! You must continually stay competitive. You must do better year after year; otherwise, the market will push you out. The logic becomes all-consuming— grow to survive. Increase profit and cut costs to survive. In this framework, wages are not ultimately about workers, especially in an economy in which people need to work for others in order to live. Instead, wages essentially boil down to maintaining the life and well-being of the worker so that they can continue working. What matters for the owner, most often, is profit.

Narrated morally, greed lies at the root of our modern capitalist system. Greed is its logic. For some, this is just an account of the way the world works. But for the Christian, this ought to be terrifying.

Neoliberalism and Finance

Two other elements inform the particular mode of capitalism that we face today. Our current economy is neoliberal and, as Kathryn Tanner has said, finance dominated.

When I say our current economy is *neoliberal*, I mean that our economy atomizes us, telling us that individual fulfillment and attainment are the most important ends. One pastoral theologian describes neoliberalism as "a cultural project," "a way of organizing human society based on the principles of individualism and competition."[5] It's best to consider this way of thinking not in terms of a particular political policy but in terms of what it says about human beings. A neoliberal economy tells us that we are fundamentally competitive, self-interested individuals. As such, anything that restricts us, whether individuals or the government, from making as much of a profit as we can is a threat.

Neoliberalism keeps us from thinking of our neighbors as neighbors. It's obviously at odds, then, with the way we have been called to live in Christ. If society is based on individualism and competition, then I am the one who matters; you matter only insofar as your existence and deeds are beneficial to me. A society built in this way keeps us from caring for and even caring about one another. How does such a lack of care practically reveal itself? Most clearly in our regard for public goods or the common good in general. The government is viewed primarily as an obstacle to "flourishing"—to unmitigated profit making. You can easily understand, then, how taxes are perceived as a burden rather than as a way to provide goods for the general population. Neoliberalism squashes communal questions, convincing us there is no good in common, only what's good for "me."

The neoliberal project also teaches us that those who suffer do so because they have failed to be competitive enough. If they had just worked harder, they would be flourishing like the rest of us. Theologian Bruce Rogers-Vaughn describes this notion as the toxic air we breathe every day, infecting us with what he calls "third-order suffering."[6]

First-order suffering is the suffering we all experience as humans: death, disease, natural disasters, and the like. Second-order suffering is the suffering that other humans inflict on us. Think of murder, sexual assault, theft, war, and oppression. The thing about first- and second-order suffering is that one can point to their causes. Much of our suffering today, however, is not of this sort. In a political economy and a culture that isolate and pressure us, the causes of the stress and anxiety that saturate our lives are hard to identify. No one person, nation, or institution is to blame. Third-order suffering is the frustration and ill feeling that students and employees experience even at a workplace or school whose policies and processes exhibit no explicit bias. Such suffering can be traced to the reality that a majority of our institutions have bought into a broader economic logic—namely, that the private is better than the public, that what matters is what one can achieve as an individual, and that one's primary relationships are competitive in nature.

It is extremely tiring to compete all the time.

Perhaps the most dangerous element of neoliberal capitalism is its relentless commodification: everything about you can make money. Your time, your body, and your talents are all possible profit sources, and if you can't find work in the marketplace, don't worry! Such assumptions lie behind much of the culture of social media influencers; you can commodify every part of your daily life if you can convince people that it is worth watching, because advertisers will pay to get as many eyes on their products as possible. Orienting one's life to the production of "good content" is a result of neoliberal capitalism.

To this neoliberal base, we have to add another component. I was a finance major in college, and in between my junior and senior years I interviewed with several investment banking firms. During that process, I realized that the Lord didn't want me to pursue that vocation after all, so I decided to apply to seminary instead. Sometime later, as I reflected on my experience, one question kept nagging me: Had I ever considered the morality of my finance studies? At the time, I was enamored with the idea of accumulating money, but I didn't consider the disconnect between profit and actual goods and services.

Financialization occurs when the financial sector, rather than, say, industrial production, dominates the economic activity of the world. Consider credit cards: we often pay for things with money that doesn't technically exist, with money we hope we'll have sometime soon. Our current capitalism is dominated by finance; people can make ridiculous amounts of money not by producing goods and services but by repackaging, redistributing, and essentially betting on complicated financial instruments.

This reality creates a supremely complex economy, one in which we don't really know where our money goes or where it comes from. It also compounds our economy's neoliberal capitalism: financialization encourages us to think even of the future as a commodity. Risk itself becomes a financial instrument. Nothing, then, escapes the clutches of moneymaking.

For people who just want to get rich, we live in a golden age. But for those who ascribe to a faith in which riches and wealth are articulated as God's greatest rival, we live in an age of horror. Ours is an age when Mammon is eager to sink its talons into our hearts and stretch its tendrils around our throats.

Greed's Favorite Scene Partner

Why would such a system survive and thrive? Why would church leaders refuse to preach against it? Why do I never hear about it from the pulpit? Why am I rarely asked to confess greed's insidious effects on my life and my desires?

The answer to all these questions is that greed works. It can make some people, especially owners, fabulously wealthy. Capitalism as we know it has already done so. The issue, however, is that wealth has to come from somewhere. Historically, the source is theft. To turn back to our history, remember that the gold and silver in the Americas was torn from the ground ultimately by people who did not live there. These resources were gathered by workers (i.e., Aztecs and Incas) coerced into acting on behalf of colonizers (i.e., the Spanish) even further removed from the land in order to allow the Spanish to accumulate more. Europeans could not offer the manpower, so they stole it. But as time went on, prolonged enslavement of Native Americans became impractical, as these natives knew the land much better than their captors and resisted subjugation. So Portugal, Spain, and other European nations essentially designated Africa as a new source of labor. In the sixteenth and seventeenth centuries, Africa's most valuable export and most sought-after commodity was human beings. This abominable trade facilitated the wealth of both Europe and the soon-to-be United States.

Greed sets the stage, but it rarely does so without its favorite scene partner, violence. Colonialism and slavery are not merely lucrative acts of theft; they are also definitionally violent. Those who could not be subjugated were most often killed because their value was only in their productivity. If a person refused to work, what worth were they to an empire that depended on their labor?

It's difficult for us to truly imagine and sit with the profound violence of the slave trade. First is the violence of being stripped from one's family and homeland, often never to see them again. It is the violence of being housed in a fort by the ocean, waiting to be ferried to an unknown land. It is the violence of being tightly packed like luggage in a ship for weeks and sometimes months, undergoing sexual and physical assault and facing conditions that could drive one to suicide. From their front doors to the shores of Western Africa, African peoples were subjected into a regime of violence.

Once that violence reached North American, South American, and Caribbean shores, it took another form, summarized by historian Edward Baptist as "the whipping machine."[7] Baptist uses this phrase to refer to literal whipping as well as to all the ways that slaveholders beat the labor out of their slaves. This violence sometimes resulted in death, revealing the self-destructive nature of the cycle: it is difficult to exploit a dead body.

But because greed is relentless, exploitation sometimes did not stop at death. Historian Daina Ramey Berry tells the story of an enslaver, William Wilson, who, after a man whom he enslaved killed himself, sought compensation from the local governor for his loss. Wilson sought to commodify this man even in death. Berry chillingly narrates the story this way: "The thought of a person's life marked the beginning of valuation, and interment or legal proceedings after death represented the end of his or her capital value."[8] Consider that reinterpretation of human value: before one was born and after one died, in the eyes and ledgers of some, one was just a number. Violence threatened to consume every moment of the life of the enslaved. This was the demonic reach of greed and murder.

But What about Race?

So, then, where did race, specifically whiteness and Blackness, enter the picture? I've narrated greed and violence first because those are the material conditions that arise prior to and apart from any justifying narrative. In the face of these conditions, no reason should suffice. But I also want to argue that greed and violence are both materially and logically *prior* to race and racism—that is, race and racism don't lead to domination and exploitation historically. Race and racism *follow* domination and exploitation.

Nothing was new about the racism that Europeans brought to American shores. Historian James Sweet suggests that European racial stereotypes were, alongside math and the Greek classics, learned during interactions with Muslims. He argues that these racist ideas were a "necessary precondition" for slavery in the Americas.[9] But we ought to consider a different ordering of events. Slavery was lucrative. In the face of significant wealth, any justifying narrative would do, and if some fabrication called race was easily accessible, why not use it?

Jonathan Tran summarizes the horror of racialized justifications of slavery well; he does so using language that we will repeat throughout this book: "The horror of racial capitalism does not lie in the notion that some identified others as less than human and so enslaved them. . . . Rather, the horror comes in the fact that slavers knew full well that slaves were human (for those with eyes to see, nothing could be clearer) and yet enslaved them."[10]

Here, Tran invokes the beast that we are called to resist: racial capitalism. *Racial capitalism* refers to the idea that the economy we know grew alongside the conception of race, tracing back, for Americans, to slavery. An economy built on slavery became an economy built on race and, in the grand scheme, an economy built on greed and violence. Tran reminds us that this ought to incite in us horror. It is not enough for us to parrot the claim that race is "a social construction." Of course race is a social construction. Most of what we encounter in a social setting has meaning that is constructed. But the question is this: *Why* was race constructed? The answer is exploitation. Tran uses the right word to describe our proper reaction: *horror*.

What Tran and others have called racial capitalism, Martin Luther King Jr. recognized as the triple evils of racism, militarism, and materialism. Two images in my mind bring these ideas together. The first is a demonic cycle of self-interest, a cycle that begins in greed and pride, continues through violence, and is justified by race. This cycle need not be justified by race, as we can find numerous reasons to exploit and dominate each other. What we do know, however, is that in our own history, particularly in the United States, society still operates with a racial lens.

The second image is a bit more visceral. The history of race is a history of death. Racism has killed in two ways: literally and imaginatively. Like those of a bird of prey, its talons rend human flesh. Like those of an invasive plant, its tendrils choke our moral, political, and theological imaginations. Race gives us a category that we can use to tell ourselves that exploitation and domination are right and normal. Race helps us explain to ourselves why some people are poor and others aren't, why some have access to decent housing and food and some don't, why hard work pays off for some and not for others, and ultimately why some suffer and others avoid suffering. But as race justifies with one hand, it mystifies with the other. If race and racial identity alone explain those disparities, we don't need to ask any more questions. And we often don't.

Later, I'll spend a lot of time with the moral imagination that we need. We ought to be conceiving of communities and ultimately a world where no one is poor; where everyone has decent housing, food, and health care; where nobody is an agent in another's suffering. But race as a justifier tells us that that's not the world we live in—that some have and some do not, often due to qualities over which they have no control. Race as a mystifier tells us that race itself is the reason for those realities. I ask that you heed the words of hip-hop group Public Enemy: don't believe the hype.

Race, Racism, and You

What even is race? This is a question that can only really be addressed after what I've just outlined: the social and economic context from which the category arose. I define *race* alongside theologian Jonathan Tran: it is an ideology that places a person in a racial category and a hierarchy in order to exploit them. It is not merely "the categorization of biological differences into natural kinds, where equity requires fair treatment along lines of diversity."[11] Lest you think this is simply a Black/white issue, racialization, as an exploitative process, is equal opportunity: if it can't find a place for you, it will make a place for you. In the United States, because of its economic founding on slavery and expropriation of land from Indigenous peoples, racialization had and still has its crosshairs on Black people in ways that are uniquely violent. But it victimizes all of us.

Adolph Reed Jr. refers to race as an "ascriptive identity."[12] This phrase draws attention to the most important aspect of racial identity—namely, that it is an imposed reality. Referring to race as ascriptive reminds us that race and its attendant ideas come from outside the person described rather than being inherent in them—that is, to say that I'm Black is different from saying that I'm from South Africa. The former calls to mind the category of race, while the latter describes my link to a material place. The former is ascriptive, a designation that doesn't tell you very much, if anything, about me. The latter at least has a particular place in mind.

The primary reason we think about one another racially is that we have been taught to do so. Children are not born with conceptions of race; they are taught. I was reminded of this when, in an effort to instill a deep and unassailable confidence in my eldest daughter when she was two, I told her that she was a smart and beautiful Black girl. She corrected me: "I'm not black, Daddy! I'm brown!" Of course, she was right. She isn't black, if *black* is understood merely as a reference to color. If race were primarily about skin color, it would be nonsense for me to call her Black. By calling her that, I unconsciously inaugurated her into an ideology of ascriptive difference. But there is another way to teach and another way to think. Contrary to popular opinion, race is not primarily about skin color but about people seeking to categorize one another in order to exploit them. It is about greed.

As Reed explains, an ascriptive identity like race "help[s] to stabilize a social order by legitimizing its hierarchies of wealth, power and privilege, including its social division of labor, as the natural order of things."[13] Note the role that race plays in our society: it tells us that things are the way they are because that is the way they are supposed to be. It tells us that poor Black communities exist because of "Blackness," whatever that may mean. "Black communities" are perceived as having common traits and characteristics, a perception that already assumes that race is inherent rather than ascribed.

W. E. B. Du Bois describes this reality in his 1940 autobiography, saying that "the black man is a person who must ride 'Jim Crow' in Georgia."[14] In this pithy saying, Du Bois underscores that Blackness as a racial designation says nothing about someone's character. Because society has declared a person to be Black, such a person is expected to occupy a certain place and follow certain rules. Such an idea goes back to the birth of modern race relations. The following definition of race comes from sociologist Oliver Cromwell Cox: Race is not about some timeless hate between groups of people. Rather, it is rooted in material exploitation.[15]

This is but one of the reasons why the claim to "color blindness" misunderstands the stakes of the conversation. To be sure, the person who claims "not to see color" is often, in good faith, trying to articulate that they do not interpersonally judge according to race. This is an admirable pursuit! Perhaps you have used this terminology yourself, recognizing that racism is bad and wanting to assure someone that you do not harbor racist ideas. Due to the social pressures of the civil rights movement, however, this is a bare moral minimum. After all, no one wants to be known as a racist! Yet one of the unforeseen consequences of a movement that placed a considerable stigma on being known as racist is that it drove racist thought underground without addressing the conditions that make racism appear reasonable.

Claiming to be color blind also suggests that one desires race to be evacuated of its power. Wonderful! I do as well. But this power is no more reduced by blindness than it is by hypervigilance. The language of *blindness* emphasizes what one does not see rather than how one interprets what they do see. It is one thing to claim not to see the color of my skin and to claim to treat me like anyone else. It is quite another to understand the ways in which the color of my skin has been imbued with social meaning without my consent (remember: "ascriptive difference") and to seek to dismantle the ways people have used it to dominate, exploit, and ignore one another. In short, we ought never use the language of *not seeing color*. But at the same time, we do not need to swing to the other side of "celebrating color." It is best to neither ignore nor celebrate race. Rather, race must be defanged, which requires that it be recognized and seen.

Many may balk at this point, particularly my Afro-American brothers and sisters. After all, racial and interracial solidarity has produced so much good fruit. Perhaps you have had life-changing personal and institutional experiences of reconciliation. Also, because white racial identity still exerts dominative power in the United States, one could argue that Black churches, colleges, and universities; immigrant churches; and other monoracial and monoethnic enclaves of support are still needed amid a hostile world. But for Christians, this reality is one to lament, not celebrate. The designation *Black* and other terms of racial identity did not arise in a vacuum. They arose out of the need for self-defense. Over time, however, a battle that was imposed in history becomes, to us, permanent and integral to our own identities. Modes of oppression appear to all of us to be natural. As Reed says, "Dominant classes operate among themselves with a common sense that understands their dominance unproblematically, as decreed by the nature of things."[16]

It is difficult to convince someone in power that the grounding for their power is shaky at best and evil at worst. Power seeks to maintain itself; giving it up seems foolish. But resisting the draw of power and decrying its abuse is Christian. If Christ is indeed our model, then domination should have no part in our lives. Monoracial and monoethnic spaces are good in a proximate sense, not an absolute sense. Building solidarity should be the goal rather than mere survival. We should want our neighbors to thrive rather than merely survive.

We won't defang racism by acting like it doesn't have power. To weaken race and racism, we have to treat them like the death-dealing phenomena they are. We don't need to be *post-racial* or even primarily *anti-racist*; we need to be *anti-racial*. Racism itself has to be consciously evacuated of its power. But even that is not the final goal. A world without prejudice would be great, but racial prejudice is not the primary problem. It is more of a cloud of smoke than a ghostly apparition; the crusade against it is not a battle against a specter that lurks ready to pounce but rather a battle against a cloud of smoke whose primary purpose is to obscure.

The concept of race is meant primarily to give the illusion of reasonability to the evils that we witness on a regular basis. Our ultimate goal as Christians, then, is actual, sweeping, life-giving justice. A world without race and racism is not the only world we want. After all, an ideology of racial difference is only one ideology among many that serve to "stabilize capitalist social reproduction."[17] Race is new in one sense but old in another. It is new in the sense that we can historically trace it, and it is not ancient. It is old, however, in the sense that it speaks to a deeper tendency as old as sin, a tendency to create hierarchies and to maintain a status quo that we see as beneficial to us. With this in mind, we ought to desire a world devoid of unjust suffering and free of exploitation and domination, a world where we all can eat, live, and share our resources without fear. Race and racism are obstacles to that world.

How Race Hides

Richard Rothstein has written a popular book called *The Color of Law*, which has opened the eyes of many to how government bodies helped create racially segregated neighborhoods in the North through the practice of redlining.[18] But the book leaves open the question of why. What if we went beyond the answer, "Well, they were racist"? If we know that race exists to justify modes and structures of exploitation, then the question we should really ask is this: Who stood to gain the most from racial segregation?

Historian Keeanga-Yamahtta Taylor reminds us that greed was at the root of redlining and racial segregation. She notes that after the Housing and Urban Development Act of 1968, the government and the real-estate industry moved from policies of racist exclusion to policies of predatory inclusion. Before that decade, Black people were kept out of white neighborhoods due to racist assumptions of unfitness. For years, Black people had been barred from building generational wealth through property, but in the 1960s, the doors to property ownership opened a bit wider. But when the market opened up, it did not open up justly. Instead, Black people faced what Taylor calls predatory inclusion: "African American homebuyers were granted access to conventional real estate practices and mortgage financing, but on more expensive and comparatively unequal terms."[19] The reason given? Black people were riskier to banks. But why were they perceived as riskier? Because previous economic exploitation rendered them so.

Black families struggled to escape this insidious market. But it worked out well for the housing industry. Banks made more money from white families and drained low-income Black families of their money as well.

One of our primary questions whenever we encounter racism in the world is this: Who stands to benefit politically or economically from racist actions? We will find that when people act out of hate, such hate does not emerge from a vacuum. Somewhere along the line, self-interest crawled into the brain of the offender. After festering, it took a new form: hate.

Taylor's book exposes the lie that "inclusion into American democracy through the vehicles of citizenship, law, and free market capitalism could finally produce fairness and equality for its Black citizens."[20] When Black people were granted citizenship during the Reconstruction period (1865–77), federal troops had to protect their citizenship in the South. Once that protection was removed, white supremacy ruled through Jim Crow. Jim Crow itself wasn't merely a set of social norms. It was the law. Even with the civil rights legislation of the 1960s, the wound rent open by racism would remain unhealed. The double-edged sword that rent it open, capitalism and greed, would not be the medicine that healed it. We should never forget that race is a category whose primary purpose in American history has been to justify exploitative labor. Our conversations about race often confuse our understandings of why things began and why they continue. We are constantly tempted to treat race as something that is inherent rather than something that is imposed, and this constant push and pull confuses and paralyzes us.

The best way to cut through the confusion is to look at racist violence when it is most naked, most brutal, and most exploitative. Normally, one would point to slavery as that example. It built the foundation of the US economy, and in the imaginations of many Americans, it was uniquely brutal. The connection between slavery and Mammon is clear and explicit. But to focus merely on racialized chattel slavery is to ignore the fact that the problem has been more widespread. Slavery, at least in terms of legality, faded with the Thirteenth Amendment. But the violence has continued. The exploitation has continued. The narratives have continued. But these three realities have not mixed in a way more violent than during the regime of racialized lynching in the late nineteenth and early twentieth centuries. I want to focus on lynching because extreme circumstances reveal one's deepest commitments. Crisis can paralyze, confuse, or foster creativity in each of us. The violence of racial capitalism can do the same thing to all of us. We are not the first to endure, and we are not the first to attempt to resist.

2

The Talons and Tendrils of Racial Capitalism

Lynchings: the crowning glory of American democracy.
—Francis Grimké, *The Works of Francis Grimké*

Racial violence has always killed in two ways: with sharp talons and with constricting tendrils. In fact, demonic powers employ both means, and I do not say "demonic" lightly. I will repeat the language of the powers, the principalities, and the demonic throughout this work because it is important to remember that our battle is never primarily with one another (Eph. 6). These cosmic powers of evil seek to kill our bodies and our minds.

Lynching itself is most recognizable as the talons: most people are shocked by it because of how openly brutal it is. While we often associate lynching with hanging, white mobs killed Black people in a variety of brutal ways. But it's also shocking because it's so *recent*. We are only a few generations removed from an era when thousands of men, women, and children, chanting racial slurs, burned human beings alive and took their body parts home as souvenirs. Many would like to think of themselves as incapable of such things, and that assumption shapes how history is told. It is easy and comforting to tell the story of American race relations in the nineteenth and twentieth centuries as a story of progress: from slavery through Jim Crow to the liberation of the civil rights movement. But one sentence from W. E. B. Du Bois pierces that reverie: "The slave went free; stood a brief moment in the sun [during Reconstruction]; then moved back again toward slavery."[1] After the Civil War, Afro-Americans enjoyed about a decade and a half in which the United States made perhaps its most significant efforts toward a multiracial democracy. Reconstruction was a period when the federal government promised, through the Reconstruction Amendments, to protect and enforce the rights of newly freed Afro-Americans. Republicans were in power in the South, and they used their influence to empower Afro-Americans and protect their rights. But then came the reversal.

Lynching: The Early Days

For Rutherford Hayes to become president in 1877 and to secure a peaceful transition of power, he had to make some agreements with Southern Democrats. Democrats were, at the time, the vocal party of white supremacy. The only way to appease them was to leave the South to them—particularly, to allow them to follow whatever racial rules they saw fit. They called it "home rule." But I hope you can see what is wrong with such an arrangement. Those racial rules would include the violent subjugation and exploitation of Black people. But sacrifices must be made to maintain power. So Hayes determined that the South could handle its own business.

The period that would follow was called Redemption. As eminent historian Eric Foner lays out, the so-called Redeemers were committed to "dismantling the Reconstruction state, reducing the political power of blacks, and reshaping the South's legal system in the interests of labor control and racial subordination."[2] What had been clear to Afro-Americans during this time became clear to all: federal intervention was the only reason they had been able to vote and enjoy a semblance of political rights. The celebration of Juneteenth today is bittersweet for this very reason: it reminds us that racialized chattel slavery did not end with the Emancipation Proclamation (published in 1863). In fact, it arguably didn't even end after the Civil War. The Thirteenth Amendment allowed a loophole for slavery if one was incarcerated, but after Reconstruction, the Redeemers seemed intent on reestablishing the racial status quo that they had enjoyed before military intervention. The US government retreated from Reconstruction's ideals in 1876, and that created catastrophic results, especially for Afro-Americans.

I tell this story because it provides an important context for lynching. Mobs of thousands, burning Black men, women, and teenagers alive, did not spring fully formed from the head of Zeus like Athena did. Lynching was lovingly nurtured by centuries of white-supremacist thought, lust for power, and, as we will soon see, greed. Remember: the economy of the South and, in a sense, the nation and the world ran on cotton plantations. Cotton plantations, however, depended on Black labor. Though such a dependence was officially taboo in the decade following the Civil War, many white people resented their loss of racial dominance. The founding of the KKK and other white paramilitary groups during the period proves this point. After 1877, a new regime of violence rose to maintain white supremacy.

Beginning in the late 1880s, lynching became an almost exclusively racialized phenomenon. Before then, mobs would occasionally operate outside or despite the law and tar and feather people accused of crimes or, in rare situations, kill them. But it was not a widespread or explicitly race-related phenomenon. In fact, Black mobs would lynch alleged Black offenders. But in the late 1880s, the number and proportion of Black people—specifically, Black men—killed in the South by white mobs began to rise. A blanket of profound evil was beginning to descend over the United States.[3]

I follow sociologists Stewart Tolnay and E. M. Beck in characterizing the years from the end of Reconstruction (1877) to the beginning of the Great Depression (1929) as the lynching era. In fact, this is the best way to characterize this period in American history: thousands of incidents in which mobs publicly and privately, cruelly and brutally took the lives of men, women, and children is era-defining. When asked why lynching occurred during this period, Southern apologists were quick to claim "popular justice" for certain crimes, specifically, some would argue, for "the one crime"—namely, rape. One cannot consider lynching without addressing the toxic soup of gendered stereotypes, sexuality, and racism.

In short, Southern apologists argued that Black men were bestial rapists who, released from the civilizing bonds of slavery, would wreak havoc on an unsuspecting and innocent white population. The prevailing image of white women stoked this fear: they were innocents, unable to protect themselves. These narratives were both false and deadly, and Afro-Americans saw them as such. The arguments of Francis Grimké and Ida B. Wells are paradigmatic of those views, as we will see in later chapters. But as to why the phenomenon began in the first place, the answer is the demonic cycle of self-interest: political and economic subjugation still had to continue. In order for it to continue, especially in a society that at least federally seemed to undermine such domination, violence and terrorism were necessary for social control. And in order to cloak naked greed and lust for power, race and its attendant lies of sexual deviance stood at the ready. Thus, lynching, in a sense, was not really new.

46

It was a violent continuation of a violent status quo. It played the role that the lash had played in slavery: the role of discipline.

Brutal, public death continued throughout the American South for decades, filling Black communities with terror. The unpredictability of lynching was the point; any breach of Jim Crow could be perceived as a lynchable offense. You didn't even have to be an offender. If you were near someone or related to someone who was accused of an offense, your life was in danger. Such a reality incited responses from Black communities, some of which we will soon see, but first, we must stare into the abyss. I want you to see and feel the extent of the regime. We must witness the violence and weep. The most recent estimate of confirmed lynchings of Black men from 1883 to 1941 numbers around thirty-three hundred, at a minimum.[4] Many lynchings were not recorded by newspapers. Some men were accused of crimes and never heard of again, only to be found dead later. Thousands of families were displaced by the threat of lynching. The rope and the stake cast a long shadow over American history.

Lynching: The Middle

In 1903 the National Baptist Convention, the largest Black Christian denomination at the time, had a problem. The previous year, author and Baptist minister Thomas Dixon had released the first book in his Reconstruction trilogy, the wildly racist *The Leopard's Spots: A Romance of the White Man's Burden—1865–1900*. Dixon wrote his book in response to Harriet Beecher Stowe's *Uncle Tom's Cabin*, which he thought mischaracterized the South. Dixon took it upon himself to champion white supremacy and Black inferiority literarily. Through his trilogy, he sought to communicate that Black people were dangerous beasts who needed to be tamed. National Baptist Convention leaders understood that Dixon's book threatened

Black life, so delegates made a formal request that one of their number write a response. That request went out to pastor and author Sutton Griggs (1872–1933). He would write one of the most sensational novels of Black literature in the early twentieth century: *The Hindered Hand*.

Perhaps the most shocking chapter in *The Hindered Hand* is the one titled "The Blaze." There, one character, Bud Harper, has just killed his neighbor Sidney Fletcher in self-defense. Once news gets out about the altercation, a mob of several hundred whites gathers and hunts for Bud, shooting and hanging Black people along the way. Bud and his wife, Foresta, flee for their lives. The title of the chapter, however, describes their ultimate fate.

After the mob catches the Harpers, they fight among themselves about where the execution should take place. One man declares, "We want this affair to serve as a warning to darkies to never lift their hands against a white man, and it won't hurt to perform this noble deed where they will never forget it. I am commander to-day and I order the administration of justice to take place near the Negro church."[5]

The mob then finds two trees on the church grounds and ties Bud and Foresta to them, piling wood around them and pouring oil on them. They cut off Foresta's hair and fling it to the crowd as a souvenir. They cut off her fingers; one man drives a corkscrew into her flesh. They force Bud to watch the entire ordeal before turning their murderous eyes and hands toward him. After torturing both of them and beating Bud so badly that one of his eyeballs hangs from its socket, they light the pyres and burn Bud and Foresta to death.

Why would Griggs add such a story to his 1905 book? Some readers would characterize it as over the top. Black readers, however, knew better. They knew that Griggs's story wasn't really fiction. It was history. In fact, much of Griggs's description of the lynching was taken word for word from editorials written in February 1904. On the seventh day of that month, Luther and Mary Holbert were murdered by a mob in the exact same fashion: burned, tortured with corkscrews, and dismembered in front of hundreds. From 1883 to 1941, thousands would meet the same fate as the Holberts.

In May 1916, the nation was shocked, a city's reputation was marred, and thousands witnessed an atrocity, the likes of which had become all too common in American life. Jesse Washington, age seventeen, had confessed to raping and murdering Mrs. Lucy Fryer, though historians still debate Washington's guilt or innocence. The events that followed make it difficult for us to determine certain facts. But we do know how Waco, Texas, responded.[6]

On May 15, Washington stood before a judge and a crowd of fifteen hundred people in a courtroom designed for five hundred. Washington seemed unafraid, as he had been told that the mob would not come after him if he confessed. The trial was short, and the jury delivered its verdict at 11:22 a.m.: guilty. The punishment would be death.

The stenographer told a National Association for the Advancement of Colored People (NAACP) investigator that the courtroom paused for a full minute. Within that minute, the stenographer and the sheriff slipped out of the courtroom. They knew what was coming, and they had no desire to see it. A cry went out from the back of the courtroom: "Get the nigger!" No one offered a hand or a word of protection. Washington was now at the mercy of the crowd. Yet mercy is one thing that race and its racist mobilization have none of.

The mob surged toward him and pulled him out of the courtroom, dragging him to a car that they chained him to. When that chain broke, the man who had yelled in the courtroom apparently dragged Washington by his own strength. On the way from the courthouse to city hall, the mob tore his clothes, cut his ear off, and castrated him, according to the testimony of a little girl. We must keep in mind that these events were family affairs. The younger generation needed to be taught how race works in American society and what happened when lines were transgressed. In fact, children were encouraged to participate, as a young boy lit the fire that would ultimately claim Washington's life.

In 1923, a man named Solomon followed his father, Oliver, from his home in Mayersville, Mississippi, to East St. Louis, Illinois. Oliver's father, Wilford, had been born in slavery, but after he became free in 1866, he sharecropped while his wife did domestic work for local white families. They were able to fully pay for eighty acres of land by 1883, a remarkable accomplishment. Unfortunately, they would not be able to keep it. According to family members, Oliver either walked away from a white store clerk while she was talking to him or hit a white man who had treated him unjustly. Both were offenses for which a Black man in Mississippi could be lynched. This led Oliver and Solomon, the Foley family, along with millions of others, to relocate from the South to the North in search of economic opportunity and freedom from domestic terror. This story and history are deeply personal. After all, Oliver was my great-great-grandfather.

These three stories are paradigmatic of the barbaric depths to which human beings will go to assert their dominance. But most of all, these examples place before our eyes the telos of race and racism: death. I have narrated only four stories so far: those of Mary Turner, the Holberts, Jesse Washington, and Oliver and Solomon Foley. Thousands more can be told. Some of them have been publicized, while many others, like that of my ancestors, have not. Activists struggled against lynchings from the 1880s through the 1930s, advocating for anti-lynching legislation, writing pamphlets, giving speeches, and talking to politicians; yet lynching numbers danced.

The worst year of the lynching era was 1892, after which the numbers dropped, with a few notable upticks. Scholars continue to discuss the reasons why the numbers spike at particular times. We will soon discuss why lynchings seemingly stopped. But for Black men and women of this period, the fact that lynching occurred less often was not a significant comfort. Its death-dealing power loomed large over their lives, reminding them that they could be singled out by violence and even swept up in it.

Lynching took not only individual lives or pairs of lives but also the lives of groups of people. Some call these events "race riots." They are more accurately called race massacres or mass lynchings. The language of *riot* fails because it suggests that the problem in view was merely the disturbance of the peace and that a level of mutuality existed between whites and Blacks. To characterize these events as riots is to rankly mischaracterize them. Whether examining the incidents in Colfax, Louisiana, in 1873; Wilmington, North Carolina, in 1898; Atlanta in 1906; Slocum, Texas, in 1910; East St. Louis, Illinois, in 1917; Chicago in 1919; Ocoee, Florida, in 1920; Tulsa in 1921; or others, we are not looking at fights that just got out of hand. We are considering massacres and spectacular public displays of violent white supremacy. In other words, such displays were, in their own way, spectacle lynchings.

Consider the 1873 event in Colfax, Louisiana, a massacre that took place soon after the 1872 gubernatorial election. One historian calls it "the bloodiest single act of terrorism in all of Reconstruction."[7] His language is apt; this was indeed an act of racial terror. Newly freed people had thrown in their lot with the Republican candidate, and while white voters sided with the Democrat, the Republican narrowly won. Afro-American residents of Grant Parish, fearing that Democrats would take the government by force, tried to occupy the county seat, building trenches around it. They were able to hold out for three weeks.

But then, on Easter Sunday 1873, the normal joy of celebrating Christ's resurrection was instead marked by the bloodshed

51

of the innocent. A white mob attacked Colfax's courthouse, and the people surrendered. Armed with rifles and a small cannon, the white mob indiscriminately murdered hundreds of Black people—280 by one count. In that act, Black people were reminded what could happen if they dared to defend themselves.

In 1906, Black Presbyterian Francis Grimké preached to his Washington, DC, congregation after the Atlanta race massacre. His text for the day was 2 Corinthians 11:24–26, the passage in which Paul boasts in his numerous sufferings—his prison terms, his floggings, his shipwrecks, his hunger, and his thirst. For Grimké, the fact that relatively few Blacks had been lynched recently was no comfort. He told his congregation, "What was true of the apostle Paul is true today of our race in this country, especially in the southern section of it. We are in constant peril; no one is safe for a moment. We are liable at any time to be shot down, to be brutally murdered."[8] We'll turn to Grimké more comprehensively in the next chapter. Here, we are reminded that each incident of racial violence snuffed out both lives and hope.

Finally, at the root of all forms of lynching was an attempt to maintain political and economic power. When we dig into the reasons behind the massacres and lynchings I've outlined above, we notice that many of them originate in arguments over wages, disagreements about political representation, and transgressions of arbitrary political boundaries—namely, Jim Crow. I mention this point to remind us that race is first and foremost about power and resources. Mobs of white men, women, and children did not gather arbitrarily to attack darker-skinned men merely because of their melanin. By the nineteenth and twentieth centuries, race had been defined and linked to political power and a presumed economic status: if you were Black in the South, you were assumed to be poor and under the political boot of white people. That was largely ensured by slavery. After emancipation, however, that status quo was upended, and it was difficult to wrest power from the hands of those who were used to wielding it.

But the most important question remains: Why did lynching stop? Was there a moral revolution? Did the activism work? Did the federal government finally step in?

The answer is simple: lynching faded as opportunities and reasons to lynch became fewer. Our racist society did not get better. It just got smarter.

Lynching: The End

Lynching ended because it became bad for business. This rather simple fact undermines how we prefer to narrate our national history. For example, consider the stories we tell ourselves about the *Brown v. Board of Education* Supreme Court ruling.

Influential lawyer and educator Derrick Bell has investigated the context of *Brown*, asking why school desegregation occurred in the mid-1950s rather than in the decades prior, when the NAACP and other organizations fought just as hard as Oliver Brown and his associates. What he found wasn't moral revolution. Instead, he found that the United States, during the Cold War, was facing international scrutiny for its nationwide racism, and as a result, *Brown* was, among other things, viewed as good press. In short, we could communicate to the world that we were still moral exemplars—after all, look at all the hard work we were doing to dismantle racism![9] While not the result of a moral revolution, the integration of schools was, in some ways, pragmatic. And it didn't yield—and still hasn't yielded— the intended results. In June 2022, the US Government Accountability Office revealed that during the 2020–21 school year, more than a third of K–12 students attended schools where 75 percent or more of students were of a single race or ethnicity.[10]

Bell's incisive and controversial arguments about *Brown* remind us to be relentlessly material when we consider the way that race works. The issue is not primarily how we think about one another. Remember: we are dealing with an insidious cycle of exploitation, violence, and racist justification. Progress is more elusive than we think. As comforting as it might be to think that political "victories" against racism evidence moral progress, the material circumstances of history suggest otherwise. Lynching is another disappointing example of that fact.

In the epilogue to his excellent book *At the Hands of Persons Unknown*, Philip Dray offers a few reasons why lynching finally ended:

> Lynching diminished for numerous reasons—changing ideas about women and their role in society, the sobering example of European barbarity during two world wars, the influence of white commerce and industry in the South, the due-process revolution in the courts that reflected a new concern for the sanctity of the person, the binding together of the nation by technology and ever-faster modes of transportation. Most indispensable to its demise was the steady pressure from the reformers and writers who never quit insisting that we were too good to be a nation of lynchers.[11]

As nice as this last sentence sounds, we can't rest in the inherent goodness of humanity or this nation. I'm Reformed and Black enough to be suspicious of those who look at American history and celebrate the visible goodness of humanity. American history is not a story of constant tension between humanity at its worst and humanity at its best; it is a story of constant tension between humanity at its worst and humanity trying to restrain itself at its worst. The phenomena that Dray identifies all likely had a part in lynching's demise, but none of those elements were primary. They each ate away at the logical fringes of lynching, but those were just the fringes.

Each of Dray's reasons dances around the edge, hinting at what lay at the root of lynching and what led to its fading. So why, by the early 1930s, did lynching fade? Ultimately, it faded because it became an economic liability. When Black men, women, and children fled in the wake of oppression, they struck a political and economic blow to the communities they left behind. As Tolnay and Beck argue, when paired with the broader economic changes in the South in the first half of the twentieth century, lynching was no longer viable and publicly accepted.[12]

Lynching was fundamentally a tool of social control, but not merely for the sole purpose of domination. White mobs also used lynching to discipline their labor. The rope and the stake were the post-slavery whip, the new threat for Blacks who stepped out of line. Such a method does not fade due to moral awakening; slavery did not end for that reason in America, and there was no reason to assume that its spawn, lynching, would end for that reason either. Tolnay and Beck argue this point elegantly: "We are not naive enough to believe the white elite experienced a revelation that exposed the 'evil' of prejudice, discrimination, and racial violence. Rather, their transformation was much more pragmatic and self-interested. They witnessed the exodus of the very population that provided their supply of cheap and pliant labor."[13]

During the Great Migration (1910–70), about six million Afro-Americans left the South and fled to the North. It was the single most important factor in the fading of lynching. When the South was hit in its pockets and when lynching became a regional embarrassment, practices changed. But this historical fact ought to give us pause. If a system like lynching faded for these reasons, what is really being said is that lynching began and continued because of greed—*and* it ended for the same reason. Those who lynched did not become more compassionate or loving. Rather, violence in the form of lynching became too costly. Once it interrupted the economic status quo, it had to go.

Tolnay and Beck's research shows that lynching faded because it began to lose its meaning. Terroristic violence is rarely senseless. The brutality, scope, and scale have a purpose. In the case of lynching, Black men, women, and teenagers were set on fire, shot to pieces, hanged to death, tortured with corkscrews, and displayed in front of Black places of worship not merely for the sake of sadism but as offerings to the powers and principalities of greed and power. Lynch mobs engaged in acts of communal discipline, signaling through terroristic violence how far they would allow Black people to go. Stories about the inferiority of Black people and the sexual savagery of Black men then provided the ballast for assuming that Black labor *should* be exploited and that Black people *should* be politically subjugated, and the cycle continued. Greed, violence, and lies danced in a merry-go-round of depravity.

Lynching has been perhaps the clearest example of the talons and tendrils of racial capitalism: killing by the rending of human flesh and by the choking of theological and ethical imagination. These talons were relentless, slashing and clawing at Black communities for decades. The tendrils wrought equal damage, convincing people that burning human beings alive was acceptable, even necessary.

Yet thankfully, lynching did not go unresisted. Many saw the evil of lynching and spoke and acted against it. They each met, however, with varied levels of success. We'll observe this reality in the stories of three individuals: Francis Grimké, Atticus Haygood, and Ida B. Wells. In these three, we will see models of both *how* and *how not* to resist racial capitalism and racial behaviors that are common even today. Grimké is an excellent example of how we might try to fight racism today with good intentions—and how that fight might fall short.

3

Lessons of Despair from Francis Grimké and Atticus Haygood

When the white man gets firmly fixed in his mind, as he will after a few sad experiences, that the Negro is not going to run, but is going to defend himself, there won't be so many lynchings.

—Francis Grimké, *The Works of Francis Grimké*

Unless potent influences can be brought to bear upon the negro race that will awaken it to the enormity of assaulting white women, the worst for both races is yet to come and the most dreadful chapters in this sad and fearful history are yet to be written.

—Atticus G. Haygood, "The Black Shadow in the South"

On April 23, 1899, in Newnan, Georgia, a white mob captured Sam Hose, cut off Hose's ears and fingers, castrated him, chained him to a tree, doused him in

kerosene, and burned him alive. Hose had been accused of killing his employer, Alfred Cranford, and raping Cranford's wife.

Reflecting on this event, Ida B. Wells states that "no other
nation on earth, civilized or savage, has put to death any
human being with such atrocious cruelty as that inflicted upon
Samuel Hose by the Christian white people of Georgia."[1]
Thousands gathered to witness the spectacle, and the white
press did what it often did by sensationalizing the victim's alleged crimes. Politicians picked up and repeated these reports.
On the floor of the House of Representatives in 1900, Georgia
congressman James Griggs described what Hose was accused
of: "A little family a few miles from the town of Newnan
were at supper in their modest dining room. . . . A monster in
human form, an employee on the farm, crept into that happy
little home and with an axe knocked out the brains of that
father, snatched the child from the mother, threw it across
the room out of his way, and then by force accomplished his
foul purpose."[2]

The problem with the account is that it was largely false and
devoid of context. Wells would find, drawing on independent
investigations, that Hose killed his employer during a dispute
over wages. Still, his brutal, public execution struck fear in
the hearts and minds of Afro-Americans across the country.
Hose's lynching and others like it sparked the creation of the
first nationwide civil rights organization: the National Afro-
American Council, an organization filled with leading Black
activists of the time such as Ida B. Wells, Booker T. Washington,
T. Thomas Fortune, and W. E. B. Du Bois. When members of
the council met shortly after Hose's lynching, racial violence
was prominent on their docket. They designated a Friday in
June to be a day of prayer and fasting for what was called "the
race problem." That Sunday was to be a day of preaching on
the topic. At least one pastor heeded that call powerfully. His
name was Francis Grimké.

Grimké's Anti-Lynching Preaching: The Causes

Francis James Grimké was born in 1850 to Nancy Weston, an enslaved woman, and Henry Grimké, her enslaver. Francis served as pastor of Fifteenth Street Presbyterian Church in Washington, DC, from 1878 to 1923, with a short hiatus in the middle of his tenure. During that time of caring for a particular community, he also became known as "one of the foremost black prophets in American Protestantism."[3] If one wants a robust example of how a Christian could substantively resist the ripping talons of racial violence, Grimké is it.

But he is not a perfect example. In fact, while his remedies for racialized violence sound robust and wise, they don't go deep enough. Grimké's story is a bit of a cautionary tale for us as we consider how to battle racism, especially when we come to see, feel, and touch its death-dealing effects. His story is a tale of sermons, three of which were preached as a response to the lynching of Sam Hose in 1899. A fourth sermon, however, preached after the Atlanta race massacre in 1906, reveals that resisting racial violence took a toll on him. As Grimké turned to self-defense later in his preaching career as a remedy for lynching, we can see firsthand what loss of hope looks like. In so doing, we clearly see the risks that come with facing racial violence and its parent, Mammon.

Grimké's first sermon in his lynching series outlined the problem as he saw it and perhaps the way that most people who were opposed to lynching saw it at the time. It boiled down to two claims: the South was a backward, uncivilized place, and it was full of racists. Grimké drew a picture of the American South as exceedingly violent and as a haven for people who react emotionally at the slightest provocation. But this was not merely a Southern problem. He also made sure to mention, in his moral excoriation of the nation, the most significant form of racialized economic exploitation at the time: convict leasing, especially "the brutal manner in which it permits criminals to be treated under that system."[4] States would profit from Black bodies by arresting them for vagrancy (not having a job) in an economy that denied them jobs, allowing individuals and corporations to continue the profit stream by using them as cheap labor. You may recall that this was the system that ultimately killed Mary Turner, a system that American journalist Douglas Blackmon calls the continuation of slavery.[5] On this note, referring to Black bodies is extremely relevant: you may cringe at such a de-humanizing phrase, and you would be exactly right to do so. The language of *Black bodies* suggests that Afro-Americans are reduced to their bodies—precisely the point of slavery and its progeny. Within slavery and convict leasing, Afro-Americans were literally treated like property and economic products. In a real sense, to the greedy in charge, they were merely bodies.

Grimké saw convict leasing as the economic instantiation of a deep moral, spiritual, and anthropological deficiency. This was most clear in what Grimké called "race hatred," a hate rooted in domination. Grimké explains: "The Southern white man believes that the Negro has a place, . . . a place in spite of whatever qualities he may develop, however praiseworthy, or whatever his achievements might be, in which he must be kept; and that is a state of inferiority."[6] Of course, it was not enough that the belief be true in the minds of racialized white people. Exploitation and domination are not satisfied to reside in the mind. Talons don't just make you uncomfortable. They rend your flesh.

So far, so good. In noting lynching's causes, Grimké saw with clear eyes. He saw the truth that at the root of racial prejudice lay a desire to dominate. But the easiest way to gauge someone's understanding of a problem is to see the solutions they offer. Grimké was sure to offer them in another sermon.

Grimké's Solutions

Titled "The Remedy for the Present Strained Relations between the Races in the South," Grimké's final sermon in his anti-lynching series revealed his own tactics for doing away with lynching. The solution was fourfold and intuitive, based on his characterization of the problems:

1. Raise the level of civilization in the South.
2. Either modify the white man's view of the Negro or get the Negro to modify his view of himself.
3. Eliminate the white man's hate.
4. Elevate the moral place of the Negro in general.[7]

Each of these remedies sounds like it belongs in a sermon, perhaps even one you might hear today. The first is essentially a call for law and order—that is, if communities would band together and hold one another accountable, lynching would stop. The second is a call to the truth: if one group says that Black people are inferior, and if the other says that Black people are human beings worthy of as much honor and dignity as any other human being, then someone is wrong. The third locates the problem in hate. And the fourth locates the problem, at least in part, in the character of the accused.

Each of these is a common and well-intentioned way of addressing racism today. We look to our communities to hold one another accountable. We see the lies of racism and assure one another that all people are created in God's image and worthy of dignity and honor. We aim our eyes at hate, seeking to excise it from our own hearts and from the hearts of those we love. Sometimes, we even look to those who suffer and paternalistically encourage them to lift themselves up by their moral bootstraps, urging one another to "do better." While such a strategy can turn into victim blaming, we should be able to sympathize with a pastor doing what he can to encourage his congregation. One of the roles of the pastor is to morally encourage and admonish their people. This was precisely what Grimké was doing.

But none of these remedies is explicitly economic. While Grimké saw clearly, he did not see *completely*. Even though Grimké framed the problem as one of domination and exploitation, it is curious that these realities are not the primary focus of his remedies. You would think that if power and money are the problem, you would solve that problem with some reference to those two issues. But here, Grimké falls into the same trap that many of us do: we see the material effects of racism, yet we address only the spiritual and mental remedies.

Consider the sermons you have heard about race or the Christian circles in which you have discussed it. How many have rested firmly in the fact that racism is built on lies and hate? If lies and hate are the problem, then truth and affection would seem to be the solution. Grimké's sustained argument in these sermons was different: the primary issues that undergirded lynching were lack of civilization and education. Thus, through moral and religious education, people could be encouraged to love one another and not believe the lies told by the salacious white media. All of this could be solved if the church stepped up. And all of that sounded compelling! Even with ongoing racial violence, Grimké could have descended into despair, but he refused to do so in this sermon, ending it with these words: "This Negro problem will be solved; and when it is ultimately solved, the Negro will have all of his rights. . . . America . . . will then be the land of the free. Its citizens, white and black alike, will be free, in the enjoyment of life, liberty, and the pursuit of happiness in every section of it. It will then be the home of the brave. Its prejudices will have been conquered, and right will have been enthroned in the hearts of the people."[8]

Even that conclusion points to both Grimké's strength and his myopia: he recognized the *political* elements of racial prejudice, but he had an underdeveloped understanding of its *economic* elements. The future he dreamed of was one in which prejudice was gone and rights were secured. But we can dream bigger. In fact, it is only by dreaming bigger that we can shield ourselves from the wide array of weapons the powers and principalities wield against us. Grimké would find out how difficult the struggle can get a few years after this initial sermon series.

Grimké's tactics with respect to lynching shifted in the coming years, and in that shift, we learn a valuable lesson about the talons of racial capitalism: such talons cannot be torn from our heads by education. Ultimately, racism is not a sin of ignorance; it is about pride and greed. Grimké had to wrestle with the fact that simply knowing about the brutality of lynching didn't stop it from happening. We must wrestle with that as well: knowing more about racism doesn't necessarily stop it. As long as it benefits anyone, especially the powerful, it will continue. Antilynching campaigns did not seem to quell lynching in those years of darkness at the beginning of the twentieth century. Grimké experienced something familiar to many others who have battled violent white supremacy: disillusionment. The risk of disillusionment attends us today. When we see how deep the rabbit hole of racism goes and how difficult progress is, despair eagerly waits to overtake us. When we come to a deeper understanding of a problem, it might not require us to rethink our convictions, but it does require a retooling of tactics.

But we don't want to go the way that Grimké went, though it is a tempting direction. Grimké's turn was from education to violence.

The Only Way to Stop a Mob: The Tendrils Get Tighter

When I refer to the tendrils of racial capitalism, I'm referring to the ways in which racism chokes us, leading us to think that our options are few. Extreme circumstances make those blinders more prominent. Fight or flight kicks in. Our sympathetic nervous system senses threat and responds automatically. That is how our bodies work when faced with immediate threat. But our minds need not work that way all the time.

Retaliatory violence lurks in the back of many of our minds as a last resort. In some of our minds, perhaps it appears a little further up in the list of resorts. When faced with something as extreme as lynching, however, it was ever in the minds of those resisting it, even Grimké's.

The events of 1906 were the last straw for him.[9] Sympathies with retaliatory violence were already in Grimké's mind in 1898, the year before Sam Hose's lynching and Grimké's lynching series. After all, 1899 was not the first year during which a Black man had been publicly burned alive.

Notably, Grimké's opposition to violence was more a matter of pragmatism than conscience. In an address titled "Sources from Which No Help May Be Expected,—The General Government, Political Parties," Grimké shows how the American government had failed to protect Black life, but he also admits that there has not been "much ground of hope from an appeal to force. The odds are against us."[10] White Southerners held the advantage in the form of tactics, firepower, and government backing. He could have stopped there, but he chose a different rhetorical option. He turned to the rhetoric of revolution, remembering the French Revolution and the revolution of John Brown, ultimately insinuating that violence is what works in these situations: "It may be necessary to startle the nation again by some terrible tragedy from its sleep of indifference to the increasing disregard of the rights of the Negro, by the same power that held him down before, and against which John Brown leveled his blow."[11] In other words, white people had to be awakened to the atrocities they committed, and the only way for that to happen would be if some of them died too.

Grimké, understanding his milieu, immediately follows this statement by saying that he is not counseling violence and that the Lord sometimes uses violence to wake people up. But ultimately, Grimké argued from the pulpit that anti-Black violence would breed bitterness and hatred within Black communities and that bitterness and hatred would eventually "have its harvest of blood."[12] Violence begets violence, and perhaps partaking in violence was the only way things would change. Grimké preferred peaceful methods of agitation. But nestled in the back of his mind was a seed that was beginning to sprout. That seed was the logic of the talons and of the lex talionis: an eye for an eye. This is one of the arms of racial capitalism—the seemingly rational violence of retribution. Eight years later, the seed would indeed sprout.

In October 1906, Grimké's tolerance for persecution and suffering wore out. His 1906 sermon followed the tragedy of the Atlanta mass lynching. White newspapers had spread unsubstantiated rumors about a group of Black men assaulting white women. In response, a mob of thousands of white people rampaged through Black neighborhoods, attacking Black people and destroying their businesses. One will notice a trend: mass lynchings did not target just people. In Colfax (1873) and Wilmington (1898), white mobs seized political power, and in Atlanta (1906), Tulsa (1921), and Rosewood, Florida (1923), they destroyed Black-owned businesses. Grimké was witnessing and responding to racial capitalism in its purest form: its economic exploitation, political domination, and violent enforcement.

Ruth Wilson Gilmore describes, in her definition of *racism*, what Grimké witnessed: "the state-sanctioned and/or extralegal production and exploitation of group-differentiated vulnerability to premature death."[13] It would be difficult to argue that these mass lynchings were state sanctioned. Then again, the state never sought trials or accountability for the murderers and vandals. Grimké had to guide his congregation through constant reminders of the violent powers of pride and greed. Almost a decade prior, he had suggested that retaliatory violence was foolish and that a comprehensive campaign of education would be adequate to beat back this death. He was mistaken. So he went to plan B: "There is only one effective way of dealing with a mob and that is to shoot it to death; to meet it in the same spirit of violence in which it comes."[14]

Grimké contemplated this sermon for ten days before giving it. It yielded his most pointed affirmation of violence. As much as he preached and believed the Scriptures, Grimké fell victim to lynching's terror and encouraged his congregation to fight fire with fire. His imagination could see only two weapons that could stop a racist lynch mob: bullets and dynamite. As Grimké stared into the moral abyss that lynching produced, he dismissed the humanity of lynchers, claiming that the only thing that would stop them would be fear for their own lives. His final word on the topic was that retribution was "sound, through and through; . . . it is in harmony with the dictates of nature, and of morality, and of religion."[15] He would maintain this position for the rest of his career.

The Vulnerability of Hope

Grimké preached for decades in the darkest period of Afro-American history. He was clear eyed throughout that period, trying to wisely, pastorally, and scripturally lead his congregation through incredibly difficult times. He saw the talons of racial capitalism (though, of course, he would not have called lynching by that name), and he sought to tear them out of the flesh and minds of the people he loved. Along the way, however, those talons sunk into his own mind. While they did not draw his blood, they did blind him with the blood of others.

Grimké was one of many Black Protestant Christians of the period who knew that they needed to resist the phenomenon of lynching. As people who live in a world that is no less violent and no less exploitative, we are faced with the same dilemma. We no longer fear mobs gathering, stripping us bare, and burning us atop pyres. But other forms of violence still strike us with fear: the loss of property, the loss of our jobs, and the loss of our lives. The racialized narratives that often undergird unjust disparities do the same work as the "Black beast rapist" story: they choke our imaginations. We are still tempted to look at our neighbors and fail to see them as human beings to be loved. We are still capable of tremendous violence.

Grimké reminds us of how vulnerable our hope can be. Grimké had significant theological training and a prolific pastorate. He spent decades caring for souls and growing deeper in his love for the Lord and his love for his congregation. He was also deeply involved in his community, helping to found the NAACP and the Niagara Movement. And yet, he still experienced an ethical and imaginative descent because his eyes remained firmly focused on injustice and suffering. His hope was betrayed by his tactics.

The powers and principalities that perpetuate racial capitalism want us to think that we can't fight them without stooping to their level. Grimké in his later life began to step toward the principalities. The next historical figure, Atticus Haygood, ran into their inviting arms.

How Racial Capitalism Warps the Imagination

Lynching is a profound example of the ways that race and racism rend human flesh. Yet that is not the only death that they perpetuate. Besides the literal loss of life, the loss of moral and ethical imagination is another kind of death. Our imaginations become stunted by the status quo.

One of the most distinct tragedies of the Scriptures is found in 1 Samuel 8, where the people of God attempt to forsake their calling. First Samuel 8:5 is a harrowing verse: the elders of Israel come to Samuel and complain, "You are old, and your sons do not follow your ways; now appoint a king to lead us, such as all the other nations have." This demand is, for the people of Israel, a kind of spiritual death: the people of God indicate that they do not want to be the people of God. Rather, they want to be like all the other nations. This move ushers in new forms of exploitation, all of which are outlined by the Lord in 1 Samuel as a response to the request; it also ushers in the death of the ethical and political imagination necessary to truly be the people of God.

While the people still live, their sense of mission seems to have died.

When racism does not kill by rending flesh, it kills by constricting our theological and ethical imagination. When we can no longer conceive of a better world, we lose something necessary to our humanity. The construction of race clouds our minds as we consider both what is possible and what is right. For example, many of us may look at the history of race in this country and see progress—from slavery through civil rights to a Black president, to draw an incredibly simplified line. But this narrative continues to ignore what race is and does. As I've argued, race is part of a demonic cycle of self-interest, both justifying and mystifying domination, exploitation, and violence. The only progress that we ought to be concerned with is progress in breaking that cycle and cultivating a world in which racial categorization has no power. This requires a distinctly Christian imagination.

Before moving to a positive historical example and a positive vision of who the church should be amid these realities, we must name our failures. We must march a bit deeper into the abyss.

The Slow Death of Paternalism

When we contemplate the worst forms of racism, we often think of the Ku Klux Klan. Such an association makes sense.

Images of men in pointed white hoods burning crosses have been intended to instill in Blacks an almost otherworldly mythology and fear.

In its first iteration in the 1860s, the Klan aimed to intimidate Black people to keep them from voting. The federal government all but shut it down in the 1870s through the Ku Klux Klan Act of 1871, also known as one of the Enforcement Acts. The act was meant to defang the Klan and other white-supremacist paramilitary groups by threat of jail time and liability to lawsuit.

As is often the case in the history of race and racism, however, if a disease is not rooted out, its symptoms return. Legislation did not erase the goals of the Klan. In the early twentieth century, the Klan gained an even wider following with a more respectable face. It called for a white Protestant America and targeted Black people, immigrants, Jews, and Catholics as threats to American life. Its message became mainstream, allowing it to create chapters in all forty-eight states in the 1920s.[16] The night riders rode in broad daylight, parading down Washington, DC's Pennsylvania Avenue in 1925 with tens of thousands of members in full regalia.

We look back now and can recognize the Klan for what it was—and continues to be—in all its bigotry. We have a harder time recognizing the other side of the coin of racist thought: paternalism. Outright hostility and the attacking of social and political rights are examples of racial capitalism's naked grabbing for economic and political power. Paternalism is when racism puts on a custom-made three-piece suit and does the same work.

Both racial paternalism and racial hostility are based on false affirmations of superiority and inferiority. The only real difference is that racist thought in the former category feels a little better. Paternalism tells you that you're actually loving someone. Paternalism says, "I'm better than you, but I'm sure

I can spare some of my excess to lift you up." The implied generosity is nice but tainted, as it comes from a base assumption of superiority. Yet this is one of the primary ways racialized thinking has been maintained; what might appear as solidarity is simply maintaining the status quo. Let's remember: We do not need to merely tweak our world. We need to imagine a new one, free of the exploitative and violent power of race. To see the dangers of the alternative, I want to offer an example of "Christian" racial paternalism.

Our Brother in Black: A Paternalist Manifesto

Atticus Greene Haygood, a white Methodist bishop, was born in 1839 in Watkinsville, Georgia, and after the Civil War his church career picked up steam. After honing his writing skills as a Methodist editor in Nashville, he became president of Emory College (now Emory University). Today, Haygood's thinking on race is viewed as progressive.[17] However, while he may have been more progressive than many of his peers, his views of race were still evil. A claim like that may sound harsh, but I want us to think precisely and sharply about the effects of racialized thinking. In doing so, we will see that paternalism kills as much as hostility does.

Haygood's initial claim to fame was his 1881 book, *Our Brother in Black*. Needless to say, the book doesn't uphold modern progressive views on race. One chapter, titled "Some Characteristics," is an extensive list of racial stereotypes and observations. Most Black people, he says, are very poor. Most are "not systematic in their plans and labors. They are not thrifty, or frugal, or economical." They love alcohol. Most are ignorant and uneducated. Throughout this chapter, Haygood uncritically notes that white people have owned much of the best land in Georgia. Haygood explains that phenomenon thus: "They have been doubly reluctant to sell lands to negroes; not

70

because they have felt unkindly to them, but chiefly because they have been afraid that negro land owners would frighten immigrants from the South."[18]

Haygood argues that Black people essentially had it great in slavery, especially with masters who, in his words, "did the best they could with an awkward and burdensome institution, handed down to them from their fathers and fastened upon them by historical, industrial, political and social conditions that they could not control."[19] The double standard drips from the page: Haygood is eager to ascribe racial characteristics to his Black subjects while shielding his white subjects from the same assumptions. After all, slavery was reluctantly maintained, in Haygood's imagination, by powerless enslavers, subject to a system that enriched them and eased their lives against their will. *Our Brother in Black* represents an imaginative failure to apply a consistent understanding of human complexity to all human beings. Africans are underdeveloped, and benevolent white people are called to lift them up—so the argument goes.

But paternalistic bile drips from that sentiment. However Haygood might have extended dignity to Black Americans, they were children in his eyes, not neighbors. Condescending language permeates Haygood's text. Here are three representative examples:

They spend their money freely while it lasts, much as children do.

They needed protection against the worst instincts of the stronger race itself; this they received through the self-interest—for slavery was profitable in the South—if not through the humanity, of their masters. . . . If it was needful for these men in stature and children in intelligence to have masters, for a time, the Southern whites made as good masters as they could have found in any country.

71

For a time the negro was looking, with the wonder and simplicity of a child watching for Santa Claus to drop down the chimney on Christmas night, for "forty acres and a mule."[20]

A tone of paternalism and white superiority can certainly be detected in these words. But we also see a rather clear-eyed reference to the greed and domination that lie at the root of racism. Absent, however, is the necessary moral judgment—that those things are evil and to be rooted out. We fall into this same trap whenever we assume that someone is responsible for their own exploitation. We also fall into this trap whenever paternalism rears its head, as it sometimes does, in our minds and in our communities. It may not drip with as much obvious poison as Haygood's, but the assumptions can remain. We must remember that the oppressed are neighbors, not children.

Haygood's theological and ethical imagination had atrophied to the point that he could claim that Black Americans were "brothers and sisters" and yet deny racial equality in every sense of the word. As much as he called for Black education and so-called brotherhood, Haygood still categorized Black people as a "national problem."[21] The point at which people themselves become a problem rather than the injustices that they are subjected to is the point at which ethical thought dies.

Unfortunately, Haygood still had breath to lose. Paternalism is not benign. Loving parenting involves discipline, often predicated on the fact that one's child is still learning the difference between right and wrong. Understood through the murky and exploitative lens of paternalistic racism, white men and women had to teach their Black neighbors right and wrong. The methods, however, were often violent. Haygood, near the end of his life, was asked to explain particularly brutal lynchings. His response would lead Ida B. Wells to question how such a man could claim to be a Christian.

From Black Brother to Black Shadow: A Defense of Lynching

Haygood was asked to explain why two Black men had been burned alive in 1893. After the worst year of lynching in American history, Haygood lamented that lynching no longer seemed surprising. But for him, the issue was not that lynching brutally and publicly took a human life. The issue was that it was *anarchic*. Haygood's most trenchant critique of lynching in this editorial was not that it was unjust but that it was uncivil. Lynching was evil to Haygood because "in organized society, there is no higher civil or social duty than obedience to law; the lyncher is, of all men, the violator of law."[22]

However, what took place on February 1, 1893, was not anarchy. It was the methodical, sadistic taking of a human life at the hands of thousands.

On that date, seventeen-year-old Henry Smith was lynched for killing the young daughter of a deputy who tried to arrest him for acting drunk and disorderly. Newspapers said the child had been sexually assaulted as well—a more horrific crime could probably not be imagined. From the data available, it's likely that Smith did kill the child, though many of the details, including the sexual assault, were likely fabricated.

Knowing that a mob was after him, Smith fled but was soon captured. The front page of the *New York Times* on February 1, 1893, had a headline nestled in its corner: "To Be Burned Alive: Henry Smith Captured at Paris, Texas." The text comprised three chilling sentences: "The negro Henry Smith, who assaulted and murdered four-year-old Myrtle Vance, has been caught and will be brought here to-morrow. He will be burned alive at the scene of his crime to-morrow evening. All the preparations are being made."[23] Like many lynchings before and after, this atrocity was planned and broadcasted.

The *Times* would begin the full story the next day with a sentence that perfectly, if inadvertently, hinted at the sadism

73

of lynching: "Henry Smith . . . has expiated, in part, his crime by death at the stake." Smith paid the price with his life and with his dignity, but if the mob could have, it would have taken more. Earlier, when Myrtle's body was found, the town gave chase. Their bloodlust would not be stopped by officials. Smith was captured and held through the night until he confessed. The next morning, Paris citizens demanded that Smith be handed over to them. He was. At noon, the prisoner's train arrived from Arkansas, where he was being held by authorities, and was met by a crowd of thousands. The crowd marched Smith all around the main city square before putting him on a scaffold, elevated above the crowd. There, "the victim was tortured for fifty minutes by red-hot irons being thrust against his quivering body. Commencing at the foot, the brands were placed against him inch by inch until they were thrust against the face. Then, being apparently dead, kerosene was poured upon him, cottonseed hulls placed beneath him, and he was set on fire. Curiosity seekers have carried away already all that was left after the memorable event, even to pieces of charcoal." The people cheered every one of Henry's screams. Not only did they apply hot irons to Smith's body, but they also burned out his eyes with them and jammed them down his throat with glee.[24]

Even as you read this description, disgust likely courses through you at both the crime and the punishment. Haygood had that same shock and responded with a chilling paragraph that merits quotation in full. How should we respond to atrocity that boggles our minds? Haygood writes:

Sane men who are just will consider the provocation. Sane men who are righteous will remember not only the brutish man who dies by the slow torture of fire; they will think also of the ruined woman, *worse tortured than he*. When they think of the infuriated mob in Paris, Texas, and the negro ruffian tortured most

74

horribly till he was dead, they will think also of a white baby, four years old, *first outraged with demoniacal cruelty* and then taken by her heels and *torn asunder in the mad wantonness of gorilla ferocity. Indeed, the instant comment of a negro man to whom I stated this case was, "He ought to have been burnt."* Men, no matter where they live or how high their personal or social development, with human hearts in them, will ask, "What if she had been my baby?"[25]

Much needs to be said about this paragraph, all of which sheds light on the ways that racialized thinking chokes Christian imagination. The first thing to notice is the invocation of *sanity, justice,* and *righteousness,* words the Christian will immediately seize upon. But the context is jarring. Haygood suggests that justice and righteousness demand that any full-throated condemnation of Henry's torture be tempered by a recognition of his alleged crime. Somehow feeling the need to explain how a mob could act with murderous and explicitly racist intent, Haygood grasps at whatever was available in his mind to impose some kind of reason on a brutal situation. One need not compare sexual assault and murder by torture. They can both be devilish evils.

Haygood then describes Henry Smith's crimes as demonic and indicative of "gorilla ferocity." This is more than a racist dog whistle; it is outright racial provocation. Framing Smith as an inhuman aggressor is a mob tactic that seeks to soften the moral travesty of lynching. Using the language of "gorilla" and "demoniacal" is a tactic of moral distancing: if Smith was a demon or gorilla, his burning was less of a tragedy. Ida B. Wells saw these comments as deliberate and malicious, having much reason to characterize them as such.

Perhaps most indicative of racial politics, however, is Haygood's calculated "negro man" reference. But this is the result of the logic that undergirds the "I have a black friend" argument.

It was important for Haygood to make the claim "Look! I'm not being bigoted when I make these claims. Even Black people agree with me! As a matter of fact, anyone with a modicum of reason would!" Purely as a rhetorical tactic, such a move could rally folks to your side. In the case of Haygood, though, both he and his Afro-American compatriot possessed an atrophied moral imagination, more shaped by the lex talionis than by the law of Christ.

Ultimately, Haygood would end his article chillingly: "Unless potent influences can be brought to bear upon the negro race that will awaken it to the enormity of assaulting white women, the worst for both races is yet to come and the most dreadful chapters in this sad and fearful history are yet to be written."[26] If Black people would just shape up, mobs would stop torturing and burning them alive.

Anti-lynching activists felt deeply betrayed by Haygood. One of Haygood's great sins was his failure to have a truly just and righteous moral imagination. His reasoning justified one segment of the demonic cycle of self-interest: the violent enforcement of an exploitative status quo. To that reasoning, he joined his authority as a bishop of the Methodist Episcopal Church, South. In justifying the talons of racial capitalism through the language of criminality, he succumbed to the thorny embrace of its tendrils.

In Haygood, we see how race and its attendant narratives both kill and blind. He simply could not consider Henry Smith as a human being—only as a Black bestial rapist. But even that was not the worst of it. All his words were based on lies and propaganda, the likes of which always attend racialized narratives. The Southern white mob did not lynch as popular justice. Justice was a smoke screen. It lynched for economic and political dominance. But a precious few saw it that way, had the courage to say it, and had the moral imagination to fight it.

Talons and Tendrils: Two Ways to Die

Both Haygood and Grimké, in their own ways, fell victim to the talons and tendrils of racial capitalism. But we ought to see the shifts that they experienced as *developments* rather than true shifts. In both, we see blooming rather than uprooting and transplanting. We see assumptions reaching their full potential. Grimké fell into the trap of attempting to out-dominate domination. But domination can't be out-dominated; it must be disarmed. Haygood fell into the trap of superiority: when you are better than your neighbor, you cannot truly love them. It's one of the most profound elements of the apostle Paul's definition of humility: valuing others *above* yourself. Both of these traps remain for us in the struggle against racial capitalism. We try to fight the powers and principalities with their own weapons, and we see our neighbors as less than neighbors.

Grimké saw the talons tearing into his people's flesh and sought righteous means to pluck them out. He saw both the violence and the political domination that the violence was meant to enforce. But after pulling and pulling to no avail, he determined that the only way to remove the talons was to take up the sword and sever the bird's foot. Even if he had managed to sever the foot, the wounds would have remained. In fact, these talons would remain embedded. By focusing so much on the claws from above, Grimké fell victim to the tendrils wrapping his imagination from below.

Haygood, on the other hand, saw the talons tear into the flesh of Black people and identified with the bird of prey. The tendrils had choked his imagination early, and he was convinced of the lesser humanity of Black people, whether it was by affirming the degradation of their humanity on the basis of the history of slavery or by devaluing their intelligence and capability through his paternalism. Grimké saw lynching as a manifestation of hate and barbarism, so his responses were to attempt to dispel the hate and civilize so-called savages through education. As time went on, he became convinced, rightly, that hate and barbarism could not actually be educated away. But he took it a step too far, arguing that if lynching were to truly stop, the lyncher would have to die. One could understand this as the "near-sighted" approach: Grimké struggled to take in the cosmic implications of his positions and the broader demonic nature of the phenomenon he was resisting. The powers and principalities of greed and pride remained hidden under the smoke screen of racial prejudice.

Haygood suffered from moral and ethical glaucoma. His vision was not just blurred, as it would be with an astigmatism, an irregularly curved eye. Pride will do that to us. Haygood was severely limited in his ability to see the situation clearly. Those who suffer from glaucoma need to be treated for the rest of their lives to prevent vision loss. Haygood's disease went untreated and unmonitored until his death. He remained, unfortunately, blind to the dynamics of the talons and tendrils. But we have to see both clearly and completely if we are to fight for justice.

But staring into the void is not the ultimate goal; rather, it is a means to an end. Like the gospel of Jesus Christ, the good news comes amid bad news. In the case of racial capitalism and its violent arm in the late nineteenth and early twentieth centuries, lynching, the bad news was quite bad indeed. Thousands of Black men, women, and teenagers were brutally killed by mobs in order to prop up an unjust political economy.

But some figures resisted both the talons *and* the tendrils and did so before lynching went out of vogue. One figure looms above them all as both myth buster and crusader; that she did so as a Black woman makes her all the more amazing. It is to the dismantling of lies and propaganda that we must now turn, exemplified in the most significant figure in the history of anti-lynching activism: Ida B. Wells. In the annals of civil rights history, no person deserves their shine as much as she does.

4

Lessons of Resistance from Ida B. Wells

> If American conscience were only half-alive, if the
> American church and clergy were only half christianized,
> if American moral sensibility were not hardened by persis-
> tent infliction of outrage and crime against colored people,
> a scream of horror, shame and indignation would rise to
> Heaven wherever your pamphlet shall be read.
>
> —Frederick Douglass, Letter introducing
> Ida B. Wells's *Southern Horrors*

Martin Luther King Jr. Rosa Parks. Frederick Douglass. Malcolm X. Sojourner Truth. Fannie Lou Hamer. Harriet Tubman. These are the names we teach our children when we think of civil rights for Black Americans. Yet Ida B. Wells rarely figures into the pantheon. This is a tragic omission: her decades of activism, beginning in the worst years of lynching in American history, set the stage and agenda for anti-lynching activism throughout the era. She saw clearly what was obscured for many, that lynching was a tool of an oppressive political economy. Once this was clear, she set her face like flint. She would battle against this violence until her dying breath, and she would do so with relentlessness, creativity, and holy fury, each of which must characterize our current struggle against racial capitalism.

Ida B. Wells: An Origin Story

Ida Bell Wells was born a slave in 1862 in Holly Springs, Mississippi. Her father became a local entrepreneur, a member of the board of trustees of Shaw University (later known as Rust College), and a Mason. But when yellow fever rampaged through the Mississippi Valley in 1878, killing Ida's parents, baby brother, and uncle, young Ida found herself with an unexpected burden. She was given two options: live with her grandmother, away from her remaining siblings but safe, or split up the family with the help of her father's fellow Masons. For Ida, neither of those options was ideal, so she demanded that she have the opportunity to work and support her five surviving siblings. Her teaching and writing career began then; her personality and resolve as a sixteen-year-old would continue into her adulthood.

Two years later, after losing her elder sister, she moved to Memphis with her two younger sisters to join her aunt, the widow of the uncle she lost to yellow fever. While in Memphis, she began to set down roots, throwing more logs into the fires of activism that burned within her. In 1883, she was forcibly removed from the ladies' coach on the train that she took to the school at which she taught, as she was told that it was for whites only. In the aftermath of the scuffle, she went to an attorney and eventually sued the Chesapeake, Ohio and Southwestern Railroad. She would win $500; however, this decision was overturned by the Tennessee Supreme Court in 1887, which only added fuel to Ida's fire.

Wells was not to be stopped. In 1889, she became the only Black woman of record to be an editor in chief and part owner of a major city newspaper, the *Memphis Free Speech and Headlight*. The years marched on, and intermittently, she would write against lynching. But her time as editor of the newspaper would prove to be pivotal, as 1892 would be the year of the event that, in her words, "changed the whole course of [her] life."[1]

Up until this time, Wells, like most people in the country, was under the impression that lynching was meant to punish horrific crimes left unaddressed by legitimate, legal means. Lynching was just regrettable popular justice, so the story went. Like everyone else, Wells believed that Black men were raping white women and killing white people with impunity, leading white communities to lash out with protective rage. Much of her writing had tonally resembled that of Booker T. Washington, as she called her Black readers to moral development and industrial education. But then a lynching happened in Memphis that bucked these theories—the lynching of a friend.

The Lynching That Changed History

On March 9, 1892, Thomas "Tommie" Moss, Calvin McDowell, and William "Henry" Stewart were shot to pieces at the Chesapeake, Ohio and Southwestern Railroad yard. A week beforehand, a fight between children had escalated into a brawl that drew in neighboring adults. Moss, McDowell, and Stewart all worked for a successful Black-owned grocery store, and white competitors resented its success. Ultimately, the above-mentioned fight served as a pretense for a nearby white store-owner to begin a race war.

The next few days after the brawl were filled with a violent back-and-forth between Memphis's white and Black communities. Hundreds of white citizens were deputized, indiscriminately arresting and jailing Black people suspected to be a part of the conspiracy, including Moss, McDowell, and Stewart. On March 9, a mob of white men broke into Moss, McDowell, and Stewart's jail cell and dragged them to the nearby railroad yard. As one historian notes, the detail with which the daily newspapers would report the brutality they suffered suggests that the reporters had been called beforehand to bear witness to it.[2]

Wells had been out of town during these events. When she came back and discovered that Tommie was dead and buried, she wrote what would be her first stridently anti-lynching editorial. From the beginning, she recognized that the most effective form of resistance was political-economic resistance: "There is nothing we can do about the lynching now, as we are outnumbered and without arms. . . . There is therefore only one thing left that we can do; save our money and leave a town which will neither protect our lives and property, nor give us a fair trial in the courts, but takes us out and murders us in cold blood when accused by white persons."[3] As historian Paula Giddings narrates, as a result of this editorial, thousands of Black Americans prepared to leave Memphis, and "the nation's first antilynching movement had begun."[4] Wells had ignited a firestorm.

This was the lynching that transformed Ida into an anti-lynching crusader. After this, she began to investigate the lynchings that she heard of, specifically questioning the lynchers' motives. She had, up until this point, assumed that lynching happened only when rape was involved. The lynching of her friend was solid evidence to the contrary. In her investigations, she even found that some situations of purported rape were incidents of consensual sex between a Black man and a white woman, a situation that many Southern whites refused to acknowledge. When she went public with these findings, the white Memphis community called for her lynching. She fled and never returned to live in the South. In the meantime, Memphis citizens destroyed her newspaper's offices. This only solidified Ida's resolve. She had determined what lynching was about: "an excuse to get rid of Negroes who were acquiring wealth and property and thus keep the race terrorized and 'keep the nigger down.'"[5] She would stop at nothing to make sure that the national and global community knew that. Seven years later, when Sam Hose was burned alive, W. E. B. Du Bois would experience a similar conversion from scholar to activist-scholar.

Any Means Necessary: Wells's Lynching Resistance

Ida insisted that resistance to lynching take whatever form it must, and to back up this claim, she presented lynching as a multifaceted phenomenon. Over the course of her life, she creatively suggested all kinds of different responses, including education, emigration, and self-defense. She did so with a robust understanding not only of the racial elements of lynching but also of its gendered and sexual dynamics. She knew that the figures who loomed large in each lynching played particular gendered roles—the roles of the white man, white woman, Black man, and Black woman. Wells tried to dismantle the intersectional framework at its core, recognizing that race, gender, and class had to be addressed together as interlocking and multiplicative structures of oppression.[6] The narratives that justified lynching had to be refuted. First, white men were understood to be patriarchal protectors of white womanhood and, more broadly, the rightful owners of political power. As Wells would repeat, the slogan of the 1868 Democratic presidential candidates still rang in the hearts and minds of many: "This is a white man's country, and the white man must rule."

Alongside this view of white men was a view of Black men, framing Black male identity as beginning in slavery and needing to be civilized through bondage. Emancipation then created a challenge for the poor, undeveloped Black male. Unable to deal with the new pressures of freedom without the oversight of white authority, he grew insolent and thus needed to be

83

repressed by any means necessary. Such a rationale justified the indiscriminate violation of Black, overwhelmingly male bodies in lynching.[7]

Wells tore apart the racist and sexist narratives that undergirded lynching. She affirmed the humanity of Black men and women and questioned the blamelessness of white men and women. In addition, she showed that only a minimum of lynching cases involved rape allegations. By investigating lynchings early on, Wells trumpeted these facts regularly, both across the United States and later overseas.

Wells's pamphlet *Southern Horrors: Lynch Law in All Its Phases* is a masterful work that dispels racist narratives, but it is also a work of practical encouragement. Wells ends her editorial pamphlet with a chapter on self-help, in which she encourages Black readers to flee from lynching communities in order to economically cripple them. Here, she beautifully illustrates her understanding of the political-economic foundation of race: "the white man's dollar is his god," and "the appeal to the white man's pocket has ever been more effectual than all the appeals ever made to his conscience."[8] As observations like these suggest, she saw clearly that the lynchers' god was Mammon and, accordingly, that the most effective way to cripple their violence was to take profit out of the picture.

Ida also encouraged the Black press to resist with information and investigation. If more people knew the truths that she had discovered, more people would defend lynching victims. Of course, in addition to these tactics, she also advocated for self-defense—specifically, for the notion that "a Winchester rifle should have a place of honor in every black home."[9] She thought violence should be an option. This was not an argument of desperation. It was an argument of sustained, relentless fervor: lynching must be stopped by whatever means necessary, and she insisted on articulating all the different means available.

The Red Record, written two years after *Southern Horrors*, suggests five remedies for the reader. First, the reader was encouraged to tell their friends and acquaintances what they had read in the pamphlet, because disseminating truth shapes public sentiment. Wells believed that if readers knew the facts about lynching, they would seek to eradicate it. Second, the reader was encouraged, every time a lynching occurred, to go to churches, missionary societies, the YMCA, the Woman's Christian Temperance Union, or any other Christian organization and pass resolutions condemning the barbarism. Third, she suggested that the "Negro problem" (the term that numerous Black leaders used to describe the struggle for racial uplift in the late nineteenth and early twentieth centuries) be narratively reframed.[10] The "problem" did not fundamentally rest on the shoulders of the Black man or woman; rather, it rested on the shoulders of white men.

Fourth, Wells noted fiercely, "It is the white man's civilization and the white man's government which are on trial." Lynching was not merely a local phenomenon with local consequences; the fate of Christian civilization was at stake. An open question for Wells was whether "the precepts and theories of Christianity are professed and practiced by American white people as Golden Rules of thought and action, or adopted as a system of morals to be preached to heathen until they attain to the intelligence which needs the system of Lynch Law."[11] In other words, did white people actually see Christ's commands as binding, or were those commands just a system to be preached to the heathen to further exploit them? She would have preferred the former, but history suggested the latter. Accordingly, the burden was on white communities not to lynch but rather to be faithful to the faith that they claimed because, rather simply, one could not lynch and be Christian at the same time. As simple as that declaration may sound to us, it yielded death threats for Ida.

Finally, Wells called people to specific legal action. A congressman had recently offered a resolution that would fund investigations of lynching, a legal measure that she thought could be effective. But she also knew that change rarely occurs apart from economic force. So she included economic protest in her efforts: divestment of capital and withdrawal of labor organizations. In so doing, she attempted to turn a capitalistic system poised for Black exploitation against itself. As she affirms in *Southern Horrors*, Black people's greatest power was their economic power, and the South wouldn't exist without it: "To Northern capital and Afro-American labor the South owes its rehabilitation. If labor is withdrawn, capital will not remain. The Afro-American is thus the backbone of the South."[12] In other words, she recognized the logic of the talons and tendrils of racial capitalism and resisted them squarely. W. E. B. Du Bois would utter similar words decades later, in 1935, in his magisterial tome *Black Reconstruction in America*. He would end his first chapter on the Black worker with these words: "Here is the real modern labor problem. Here is the kernel of the problem of Religion and Democracy, of Humanity. Words and futile gestures avail nothing. Out of the exploitation of the dark proletariat [or working class] comes the Surplus Value filched from human beasts which, in cultured lands, the Machine and harnessed Power veil and conceal."[13]

With words like these, Du Bois underscored the notion that slavery fueled the Industrial Revolution. The exploitation of Black workers produced the wealthy base of the American economy. In her consideration of lynching, Wells saw that historical fact as more than history: it was her present. The demonic cycle of self-interest that started and maintained slavery, lynching, Jim Crow, and all forms of racialized violence—whether aimed at Black people, Chinese railroad workers, or Mexican immigrants—presented a complex issue that required a panoply of solutions. Wells pursued them all.

What Does This Mean for Us Today? The Importance of Clear Sight

Ida B. Wells exemplified an alternative way to think about and respond to lynching and racialized violence as a whole. That alternative began with clear sight. If we are to battle the exploitation, violence, and lies of racial capitalism today, we must do so with eyes wide open.

After her friend Tommie Moss was lynched, Wells was intent on interrogating lynching as deeply as she could, and she did so with 20/10 vision—exceptional acuity. She refused to accept the common racial, gendered, and sexual narratives. As a student of sociology, she demanded that such narratives actually be backed by fact, but they were not. She constantly trumpeted the facts that greed and political domination were at the core of racial violence and that much more was at stake than the individual guilt or innocence of any lynching victim.

Political theorist Naomi Murakawa calls these insights some of the most significant things that we can learn from Wells's legacy, especially in a world and a nation that still prop up the myth of Black criminality.[14] Wells refused to accept the idea that as long as one can prove that someone is guilty of a crime, anything can be done to them. When lynching was conceived of as punishment, the only question that some asked was whether victims did something to deserve it. The proper moral imagination saw the brutality of lynching and concluded that no human being was worthy of it. Wells not only readjudicated every lynching but also indicted the very system that made lynchings appear reasonable.

Her relentlessness, creativity, and righteous fury undergirded her life's work. Despite setbacks and an onslaught of racialized violence, Wells had an almost supernaturally indefatigable spirit. She investigated lynchings for decades, submitting each one to meticulous study, and she did so creatively, mining newspapers and interrogating their accounts. She knew what to look for. Knowing that the lust for money and power lay at the root of lynching, she scoured the white press with that assumption in mind. Defenses of lynching withered under her assault, as she sought to land blow after blow against an unjust system.

That system was racialized capitalism. Murakawa summarizes it well: Wells "was a scholar of the law's continual repurposing as an instrument of white capitalist and patriarchal violence."[15] While the exploitative violence of lynching might be dealt with in one form, it would pop up in another. Abolition opened the way for convict leasing. The tortures of slavery inspired the tortures of lynching. When the violence of both sickened enough people, laws changed in order to hide the brutality. Wells witnessed some of these changes, as spectacle lynchings began to recede in the 1910s and 1920s and policing as we know it began to take its place. But her work did not stop, because she knew the main issue with lynching wasn't ultimately its anarchy and lawlessness. The problem was not that lynching did not conform with the will of the state. Instead, lynching was merely evil as a manifestation of lies, theft, and death.

Wells would die before lynching ceased in the forms that she knew. But still, the logic of that manner of violence remained. Greed was not defeated. Nor was pride. Those sins remained—and they remain to this day, saturating our current political economy.

It is time to look to our present: to the communities we find ourselves in now, to our families, to our churches. While thousands no longer gather to hungrily collect the ashes of burnt Black bodies, we must not forget the logic of Mammon worship. Mammon demands human life. As Ida says, the white man's dollar is his god, and that idol tempts each of us now. The question is whether we will organize ourselves to continue to pluck ourselves and our neighbors from that god's toothy maw. We must, and we can do it in three deeply practical ways.

Against Haygood's paternalism and the greed that truly lies at the root of racism and racial violence, we can build communities of *deep economic solidarity*.

Against Grimké's assumption that domination must be out-dominated, we can build communities of *creative anti-violence*.

And in keeping with Wells's indefatigable commitment to the truth, we can build communities of *prophetic truth telling*.

PART 2

WHERE DO WE GO FROM HERE?

5

Solidarity or Greed?

> Blessed are the poor and those who share the outlook of
> the poor, for theirs is the kingdom of God.
>
> —C. René Padilla, *Mission Between the Times*

History is most useful when it reminds us of our need
to love each other and when it gives us resources to do
so. The history of lynching is but a moment in the history of racial violence. That history has never receded from the
imaginations of Black people. It constantly reminds all of us
what we are capable of doing to each other. Race pushes us to
have deeply material conversations: conversations about money
and conversations about power. We shouldn't only *think* rightly
about one another, though that is important. More important
is that we treat one another rightly. Recognizing one another's
humanity is just one step in the process. The ultimate goal is
love.

The enduring question for all of us is one of application. If
race and racism indeed are at the helm of a regime of violent
death, a regime most explicit in the history of racial violence,
how should the people of God respond to this reality? At base,

we, as the people of God, should be consistently and relentlessly nonviolent. Some may think this ideal implies passivity, but nothing could be further from the truth. In fact, the Christian ethic is best described not as nonviolent but as *anti-violent*, characterized by the refusal to believe that killing one's enemy is ever the way forward. Our Savior's most difficult words to us are in the Sermon on the Mount, especially in Matthew 5:44: "Love your enemies and pray for those who persecute you." At the very least, killing our enemies does not fit that paradigm.

I want to be very clear about these words, precisely because of the nature of the violence that race and racism perpetuate. One will remember: racism is part of a cycle that begins with political and economic exploitation. Greed and lust for power easily consume the human mind and train us to forget about our neighbors' humanity. As this process continues, we are reminded that being exploited and dominated is not a pleasant experience, and in order to continue to exploit and dominate, violence and coercion become necessary. As we reckon (or do not reckon) with this reality, we construct narratives that bolster the status quo. Race functions as one of those narratives—an illusion that hides deeper political and economic machinations. But all of this materially leads to death.

Accordingly, the mere resistance of violence will never be enough. We have to actively conceive of another reality. The prophet Isaiah tells the people of Israel about a future in which peace will be their governor and well-being their ruler, a future in which they will no longer experience violence, ruin, or destruction (Isa. 60:17–18). Our world, however, is saturated with economic exploitation, violence, and lies. If this is true of the world and its logic, then the Christian, as a citizen of the kingdom of God and herald of the resurrected Christ, is called to bear witness to a different, redemptive way. That way requires three practical responses to the three elements of the demonic cycle of self-interest: economic solidarity, creative anti-violence, and prophetic truth telling.

These responses are not optional for the church. As we will see later in this chapter, they flow directly from the commands of Christ. Insofar as we have failed to bear witness to Christ's expectations of his people in the world, we have failed to show the world what Christian community truly is.

First, to resist economic exploitation, *Christians are called to live in economic solidarity with one another.* We are called to live generously, but generosity is not the *primary* lens through which we understand the political economy of the kingdom of God. Remember: when I use the term *political economy*, I'm referring to a particular account of resources, their distribution, and the power dynamics inherent in human interaction. The kingdom of God, as a true kingdom, has politics and an economy, yet both are characterized by solidarity. *Solidarity* more accurately encapsulates what Christ has done for us and who he has called us to be. Moreover, the solidarity we are called to results in uplift rather than dependence. A solidarity that results in dependence, along with a shallow view of generosity, maintains the status quo. By contrast, Christians and the community they are a part of bear witness to a new world.

Remember the failure of Atticus Haygood. Pride and greed are both significantly undermined by true solidarity. I cannot conceive of myself as better than you if I am walking alongside you, suffering with you. It is also much more difficult for me to exploit you and to languish in luxury when I am walking alongside you, suffering with you. Paternalism has no place among the people of God.

Breaking the First Arm of the Cycle: A New Philanthropy

Greed is perhaps the most dangerous of all the sins that tempt us. Greed is the chief of the vices. The New Testament warns us about this sin more than any other. Ananias and Sapphira are smitten by the Holy Spirit for their lies and their greed (Acts 5:1–10). Judas betrays his teacher for money (Matt. 26:14–16, 47–50). Paul warns us multiple times that the love of money has kept people out of the kingdom and that we are to put greed to death (1 Tim. 6:9–10; Col. 3:5). Greed is the paradigm of sinful sensuality and a marker of a futile mind (Eph. 4:19). Greed is the kind of thing that ought not even be named among the people of God (5:3). Greed is a form of wickedness among people who have forsaken the Lord (Rom. 1:29). James reminds us that the rich oppress and exploit, as that is what greed does (James 2:5–7). The author of Hebrews reminds us to resist the love of money (Heb. 13:5). Peter warns us against greedy false teachers (2 Pet. 2:3). But the New Testament figure most concerned about greed is the Son of God himself. Jesus warns us multiple times, whether in parables (e.g., Luke 12:13–21; 16:19–31) or through explicit commands and teachings:

> Watch out! Be on your guard against all kinds of greed; life does not consist in an abundance of possessions. (Luke 12:15)

> What comes out of a person is what defiles them. For it is from within, out of a person's heart, that evil thoughts come—sexual immorality, theft, murder, adultery, greed, malice, deceit, lewdness, envy, slander, arrogance and folly. (Mark 7:20–22)

> Woe to you, teachers of the law and Pharisees, you hypocrites! You clean the outside of the cup and dish, but inside they are full of greed and self-indulgence! (Matt. 23:25)

This is but a sampling of the New Testament's warnings against greed. The most significant of them comes in the Sermon on the Mount. When Christ explains to his disciples that laying up treasure in heaven means giving to the poor, he tells them that it is impossible to serve two masters. In our moral imaginations, we can probably envision a number of rivals to the one true God. Here, Jesus is concerned with only one of them: "No one can serve two masters. Either you will hate the one and love the other, or you will be devoted to the one and despise the other. You cannot serve both God and money" (Matt. 6:24).

Money. Mammon. Riches. All names for the same rival god, the service of whom the Scriptures call greed. Mammon lies at the root of lynching, of racial violence, of racial capitalism, and ultimately of the very concept of race itself. The demonic cycle of self-interest cannot be broken personally, communally, or cosmically without reckoning with greed. Those who are best positioned to spearhead this reckoning are those who serve the God of the Scriptures.

The best way to combat greed, envy, and their systemic counterpart, exploitation, is through philanthropy. By *philanthropy*, I mean the actual love of humanity, even though when we think about that word, we tend to think about lavish generosity. I am very intentionally not saying that the opposite of exploitation is generosity because generosity, while good, can be one sided. It can easily turn into paternalism. Our vision of philanthropy, often hearkening back to Andrew Carnegie, Cornelius Vanderbilt, John D. Rockefeller Jr., and their ilk, is often limited to thinking about only generous donations to good causes. We don't often consider that those donations often come with strings attached: ways in which the giver maintains control and sometimes gains power (or significant tax benefits). The philanthropy I have in mind to rebut the demonic cycle of self-interest is not that kind. Rather, I invite you to consider a different kind of philanthropy: divine philanthropy.

The incarnation is described in John 3:16 as a gift. We are told that God loved the world in a very particular way: he gave his Son. The nature of this philanthropy, this divine love for humanity, is such that it did not leave God unchanged. Now, before the classical theists get mad, I should clarify that I'm not saying that the nature of God changed. What I am saying and what every Christian would affirm is that there was a time when the Son of God was not human. The Son took on flesh. He became human. He assumed the form of a servant. He emptied himself as an act of generosity.

In human philanthropy, givers can give from a distance, keeping a position of so-called superiority while receivers remain in a position of so-called inferiority. That is not the kind of giving that Christ calls us to, nor is it the kind of giving that he exemplifies at the cross.

Instead, when we see our brothers and sisters in need, we are to give in a way that brings givers and receivers together, mimicking divine philanthropy. *Solidarity* is another word to describe this reality, but this solidarity has a particular purpose: equality. This is Paul's focus in speaking to the Corinthian church in 2 Corinthians 8. To borrow controversial language, Paul is not talking about equality of opportunity. He's talking about equality of outcome, which characterizes the eschatological kingdom. This kingdom is a kingdom in which everyone has what they need and has enough to share. It is depicted as the mountain of the Lord in Micah 4:4: "Everyone will sit under their own vine and under their own fig tree, and no one will make them afraid." After appealing to the Corinthians to give to their poorer Macedonian brothers and sisters, he makes two profound theological moves, an appeal to Christ and an appeal to equality.

Appeal to Christ: A Different Kind of Solidarity

Second Corinthians 8:9 says, "For you know the grace of our Lord Jesus Christ, that though he was rich, yet for your sake he became poor, so that you through his poverty might become rich." Paul frames Christ's material humiliation in the incarnation as an act of solidarity that uplifts the human race. Egyptian theologian Cyril of Alexandria says it nicely: "Christ took what was ours to be his very own so that we might have all that was his."[1] Said more pithily by Saint Athanasius, "[Christ] was incarnate that we might become god."[2] This summary of the gospel, understood by our Orthodox brothers and sisters as *theosis* or deification, reminds us that Christ became poor in order to make us rich. Christ has called us into a deeper relationship with the Godhead than we could ever imagine. This claim goes far beyond our net worth. Faith in Christ and obedience to his commands by the power of the Spirit actually substantively change us. Similarly, the way we are called to give to our brothers and sisters, mimicking divine philanthropy, is a way of giving that requires sacrifice. And this giving actually changes us and our material positions.

Here, we must remind ourselves of what we mean when we call ourselves Christians or followers of Christ. The Son of God took on flesh fundamentally to bring us into fellowship with himself and into the divine life. This is what the language of sanctification points to: even more than being set apart for God's purposes, sanctification involves us being actively made like Christ. I cannot stress the cosmic wonder of this reality enough: Christ's intention is to share everything he has with us. He shares his Spirit with us, he shares his very life with us, and, ultimately, he—the one with the most power to hoard—seeks, instead, to share his reign with us. We often think about the ancient hymn of Philippians 2:6–11 as an ode to the humility of Christ, who humbled himself even to the point of death on a cross. But it is also a hymn about Jesus's refusal to entertain any kind of greed. Instead of seeing equality with God as a resource to be hoarded for personal benefit, he humbled himself in order to share that very resource (though remaining as he was and without changing our natures, as our Orthodox brothers and sisters remind us). This is the mind-shattering message of Revelation 22:4–5 and Daniel 7:27: the Son's servants will both see him and reign alongside him.

Economically, this means that we must think about our money and possessions as resources to share rather than to hoard. In doing so, we look to the early church as normative rather than as a historical anomaly. After the Holy Spirit descended on those proclaiming faith in Christ, those communities were set apart by the four characteristics of a Spirit-filled community: devotion to the apostles' teaching, the fellowship, the breaking of bread, and prayer (see Acts 2:42). Three of these characteristics are self-explanatory: Christians believe what the apostles say as ambassadors of Christ, Christians eat together, both in shared table fellowship and the regular celebration of the Eucharist, and Christians pray. But what is "the fellowship" (Greek *koinōnia*)? Frankly, it is sharing, particularly of possessions.

Luke makes this clear in Acts 2:44–45: "All the believers were together and had everything in common. They sold property and possessions to give to anyone who had need." But the second time he mentions this state of affairs, two chapters later, he adds a detail that highlights the significance of such a concrete, material commitment: "All the believers were one in heart and mind. No one claimed that any of their possessions was their own, but they shared everything they had. With great power the apostles continued to testify to the resurrection of the Lord Jesus. *And God's grace was so powerfully at work in them all that there were no needy persons among them*" (4:32–34, emphasis added).

This last sentence is paradigm shattering. Luke is pretty clearly linking God's power to a particular arrangement of people and how they manage their material resources. But it is not unprecedented. In Walter Brueggemann's amazing book on money, possessions, and the Bible, he argues convincingly that "the Bible is indeed about money and possessions, and the way in which they are gifts of the creator God to be utilized in praise and obedience."[3] That is, one of the Lord's primary concerns for us is that we *economically* reflect his heart. And God has told us this on numerous occasions. Brueggemann finds Deuteronomy 15:4–15 to be "at the heart of biblical teaching about money and possessions, a regulation that wealth is held provisionally and debt cannot become a permanent lever of the economy."[4] In this passage, the people of Israel are told that if they do as the Lord commands, regularly forgiving debts, releasing their slaves, and caring for the needy among them, they will have no needy people. But why is this such an important set of commands, and what is God's grounding for making such demands? Deuteronomy 15:15 reveals the answer, as well as the consistent reason for most of the Law: "Remember that you were slaves in Egypt and the LORD your God redeemed you. That is why I give you this command today."

This text highlights God's argument that a just system doesn't relieve individuals from caring for the poor. Some may assume that a social safety net will discourage God's people from caring for the poor. Yet the Lord, after establishing an infrastructure and law that would eradicate need if obeyed, tells his people "not to harbor this wicked thought: 'The seventh year, the year for canceling debts, is near,' so that you do not show ill will toward the needy among your fellow Israelites and give them nothing" (Deut. 15:9). Said another way, even if a system is in place to robustly care for the poor, every member of the people of God is to be individually and communally devoted to the poor's flourishing. In that way, the Old Testament describes a communal infrastructure that cares for the poor as well as individuals who are openhanded regardless of the structure they find themselves in. A liberated people seeks to liberate others.

A people redeemed by God participates in a redeemed economy, regardless of the state government they are under. An economy of solidarity has always been an intended material response to God's gracious gift to us. Not only is such a life legislated in Deuteronomy, but it is also promised through the prophets. When Micah describes the eschatological mountain of the Lord's temple, the physical manifestation of his presence, he describes a world empty of war (which we'll discuss later) and one where "everyone will sit under their own vine and under their own fig tree, and no one will make them afraid, for the LORD Almighty has spoken" (4:4).

As Michael Rhodes, Robby Holt, and Brian Fikkert note, Micah sees that God's kingdom will be a place where everyone has access to the means of production—meaning that "each person will have an economic stake, an economic place to stand, an economic place to steward."[5] The kingdom of God is a place of true equity. The church, the community whose one purpose is to bear witness to the kingdom, is supposed to be that kind of place. The church is meant to be a community in which no one has economic needs, because the people of God see their resources righteously, as gifts to be shared.

Perhaps this means that you and your community consider operating in some or all matters with a common purse, as the early church did. But even if you do not do that, all followers of Christ are to think creatively about how they can bear witness to a kingdom economy in which everyone has enough and something to share. At the least, this ought to be said of our churches, and our churches' finances must reflect this priority. When we make this our priority, we bear witness to Christ's work, especially his solidarity with us in his incarnation, life, death, and resurrection. In this sense, truly, Christ's poverty becomes our communal riches.

Appeal to Equality: No Rich and No Needy

Paul's second move in 2 Corinthians is to appeal to equality. How many times have you heard appeals to generosity that still allow the rich to remain in the lap of luxury? In the back of our minds, generosity can even become a reason for greedy accumulation: if I get more, I can give more. Given that logic, my accumulation has no limit; the Christian can desire to be a millionaire or even a billionaire as long as they give a significant amount of their income. The Son of God explicitly grinds that ambition into the dust.

In Luke 12:16, Jesus begins to tell a parable known as the parable of the rich fool, but it is immediately preceded by the command "Watch out! Be on your guard against all kinds of greed; life does not consist in an abundance of possessions" (12:15). You will notice that Jesus cares a lot about greed. He warns us against it incessantly. In this parable, a rich man has an especially abundant harvest, and since his barns aren't big enough to hold the excess, he decides to tear them down and build bigger ones. But God responds to him soon after that thought, telling him that he is a fool and that he will die later that day. The moral of the story according to Christ: "This is how it will be with whoever stores up things for themselves and is not rich toward God" (12:21, slightly modified).[6] Our good friend Basil argues that because we properly earn nothing, we're also not entitled to anything. He describes the rich as those who "seize common goods before others have the opportunity, then claim them as their own by right of preemption." Then he offers his solution: "If we all took only what was necessary to satisfy our own needs, giving the rest to those who lack, no one would be rich, no one would be poor, and no one would be in need."[7]

The imperatives of the kingdom of God are not pie in the sky but *realistic*. To those who would say that obedience to them is impossible, we must respond, "It has been done before, and it can be done again." Our current system tells us that some must be rich and some must be poor; sometimes, we even claim Jesus's words that the poor will always be among us as normative rather than as a call to action. Jesus is saying here that until he returns, we will always have justice to seek and poverty to eradicate. But the only way to seek justice and eradicate poverty is with a vision of a world and a community where justice and the eradication of poverty are real.

This, then, is also the way to fight the material, exploitative effects of race and racism, for equality banishes exploitation. Exploitation convinces me that I ought to have more than you, and its attendant principalities contrive reasons and narratives that justify that to me. As a follower of Christ, I must respond with a resolute commitment to love you as I love myself and to seek that your needs are met as much as mine. In other words, we need to acquire a deep discomfort with inequality. We must never accept it as natural. This means that when we look at our cities and towns, often segregated racially and economically, we must not say, "That's just the way things are. It can't be changed." Instead, we have to say, "We made it this way. We can make it something else." The first step to creating change is remembering that change is possible because gross inequality is not natural. It is historically contingent.

You and I are called to be apostles of equality. Paul narrates this calling explicitly in 2 Corinthians 8:13–15: "Our desire is not that others might be relieved while you are hard pressed, but that there might be equality. At the present time your plenty will supply what they need, so that in turn their plenty will supply what you need. The goal is equality, as it is written: 'The one who gathered much did not have too much, and the one who gathered little did not have too little.'" Notably, these verses include two of only three instances of the word for "equality," *isotēs*, in the New Testament. The third is in Colossians 4:1, where Paul commands slaveholders to provide their slaves with what is right and *equal*. Many books have been written about Paul and slavery, but Colossians 4 alone gives us enough to argue that perpetuating racialized chattel slavery is fundamentally contrary to a life lived in obedience to Christ. Paul's overriding concern for equality is one of the most powerful reasons why, rightly read, Paul can be understood as an abolitionist. Any system that is resistant to deep and equal relationships is to be dismantled in the name of Christ.

Is All This Just Marxism in Disguise?

Now I have to address the elephant in the room. If you weren't calling me Marxist before, you probably are now. But I am saying that an economy of solidarity is the economic paradigm that ought to shape life within the church. Yes, Karl Marx as an economist was right about much: our current political economy *was and is* indeed built on the backs of the exploited.[8] The demonic cycle of self-interest has to start somewhere, and it starts with theft, the first stage in capitalist accumulation. Yes, Marx is right that ideology offers a smoke screen for that exploitation, as I have laid out repeatedly. Race, as an ideological lie, serves a purpose: it grabs your face and turns it away from the specifics of human suffering and instead focuses your eyes on the distraction of color. The answer is indeed to focus on the material and to resist capitalism's encouragement to forsake one another for the sake of profit.

But Marx does not have a monopoly on socialism or on a communalist economy, nor did he make those systems up. The fact of the matter is that we see socialist and communalist economies in the Scriptures. What I mean by this statement is that God continually shapes his people into a people who center their lives around care for one another rather than self-interest. Our resistance to capitalism should come from our commitment to Christ and our guarding against the very things he continually tells us to guard against. The item at the top of that list is greed; the Scriptures, both Old and New Testaments, remind us over and over again to flee from it. The revolution that we bear witness to is the revolution of the cross, the very thing that the Lord has used to shame the powers and principalities. That is the weapon of our warfare.

The world cannot operate in alignment with the kingdom before the Lord returns, regardless of how optimistic some of our brothers and sisters may be. It would be unfair to expect righteousness from those who are not united to Christ. But it is entirely fair to expect it of those who are—namely, the church. Surely, our world would be more just if the resources of any single nation were focused squarely, wisely, and robustly on lifting up the needy and dignifying the suffering. But we shouldn't expect any earthly nation to comprehensively do that, as much as we ought to mobilize whatever political power we have to support that work.

You may ask, "How does all of this affect the way I give outside the church?" or "How can I resist the exploitation that continues in my state, my nation, or the world at large?" These are good questions. What I offer here is an answer to them: the church, as Christ has constructed and called it, is meant to be an answer to these questions from the bottom up. People will know alternatives only if they see them. The best way forward is to focus on those who can do what I am suggesting, and those people are specifically those who have been indwelt by the Holy Spirit. Some assume that the Christian cultural mandate is to embed oneself in the world and to weave the threads of Christian influence, individually, into the major sectors of secular life. But the Sermon on the Mount suggests a different approach. Addressing *communities* of faith, Jesus calls the people of God to be a light to the world and the salt of the earth *collectively*, bearing witness *as communities* to alternative ways of living and being in the world. When the first church began that work, one of its first and most distinctive elements was its Spirit-empowered economic solidarity. That economic solidarity is the first line of defense against the talons and tendrils of racialized capitalism.

How Can This Look among Us? Preaching, Practice, and Politics

What would an anti-greed witness look like among us now? I'll offer a few suggestions, though such suggestions are always open-ended and to be considered both individually and communally. Economic solidarity must manifest itself in our preaching, our practice, and our politics.

Some say that we should never bring up money, politics, or religion in regular conversation. I insist that we talk about all three when relevant, because they are intimately connected. If I am to walk alongside you economically, I have to know where you stand religiously and politically. For those of us who preach, we are to preach the Scriptures according to their own emphases, and one unavoidable theme is the insidiousness of greed and the redemptive nature of the divine economy. In a world that tells us that greed is good and that accumulating wealth and possessions is benign, the Scriptures must be constantly brought before the minds and hearts of the people of God. Too often, I have heard from members of or visitors to my church that they cannot remember the last time they heard a sermon about greed. American Christianity sometimes looks like an attempt to prove Jesus wrong when he says we cannot serve God and Mammon. Let it not be.

Our daily practices ought to be saturated with philanthropy. Greed tells us that what we have is ours for our use and for our self-indulgence. Christ tells us that everything we have is a gift of God's grace and thus a tool for God's glory. This includes our time, our talent, and our treasure. Time is not merely a profit-making tool. Time is a resource that our suffering neighbors need from us. Our talent is not merely a profit-making tool either. It is a resource that our suffering neighbors, our brothers or sisters, need from us as well. Capitalism tells us that every dollar of ours should be subject to the laws of compound interest, encouraging us to store up our treasure in places where it can compound day after day, week after week, month after month. Unfortunately, those places are places where moths and vermin destroy and where thieves break in and steal. To the contrary, as Jesus commands us in Matthew 6:20, we ought to "store up for [ourselves] treasures in heaven, where moths and vermin do not destroy, and where thieves do not break in and steal." In Luke 12, Jesus tells us exactly what that means: to give to the poor and the needy. The most practical way to resist greed is to recognize that the greatest return on our investment comes from our investment in the poor. As much of a return as the stock market may offer, Proverbs tells us that "whoever is kind to the poor lends to the Lord" and that our God always pays his debts (19:17).

But we ought to restrain our greed even here. I am not suggesting that the way to get rich is to give to the poor. The desire to get rich in and of itself is the love of money and something to reject. That desire, Paul warns us, can keep us out of the kingdom or cause us to flee from it when we encounter Christ. It keeps the rich young ruler away from the glorious riches of salvation; we must be diligent that it does not keep us from the same. Solidarity with the poor brings us closer to the Lord. It purifies our intentions and illuminates our souls, shaping them to be in line with the mind and heart of God. Our giving to the needy is not only an act of obedience but also a step of sanctification and deification. When we express the kind of philanthropy that mirrors divine philanthropy, we come to a deeper understanding of God's own heart. God then uses these habits to shape us into the image of Christ, drawing us ever closer to himself. Greed and self-interest have no part in this process.

But this emphasis on practice, sanctification, and deification may nag at the good anti-legalist Protestants among us. Why all this obedience talk when Jesus is about grace? Well, Jesus is actually about obedience—obedience *enabled by* grace. He says, "If you love me, keep my commands" (John 14:15). We do not earn God's favor by living lives that resist the principalities of greed and self-interest. But by the power of the Spirit, we are the ones who *can* obey. Still, the only life that truly makes sense for us is a life of rigorous obedience to a God who knows what is best for us and who has prepared a marvelous, sinless future for us. Sanctification and deification are indeed gifts, but they are also, in an important way, cooperative works, ways in which God wishes to work alongside us.

Finally, this resistance to greed must manifest itself in our politics. The only reason why the Lord gives us resources, power, authority, and influence is so we can use it all to benefit the needy and those who have been stripped of power. In fact, an even better use of power and authority is to share them. Christ himself gives us this paradigm. When James and John ask to sit at Christ's right and left hands when he enters his glory, he refuses them for two reasons. First, he says that these are not positions that he can grant. But he also says that their request exemplifies a deficient understanding of power. Ambition has led them to seek positions of prominence. Jesus condemns this approach as a model for the faithless: "You know that those who are regarded as rulers of the Gentiles lord it over them, and their high officials exercise authority over them. Not so with you" (Mark 10:42–43). The primary purpose of power is, for Christ, service. He has come not to be waited on but to wait on others. His incarnation is an act not of domination but of divine service. In a mind-shatteringly gracious miracle, the Creator of the universe has given his life to save rebellious humanity, using his unimaginable power to exalt his brothers and sisters.

If this is what the Son of God has done with his infinite power, what then should we do with our political influence, measly as it may be? That power is to be mobilized for the same purpose: in service of the poor, the needy, the widow, the orphan, the marginalized, the immigrant, and the oppressed of all designations. Whereas our most common political question is "How will this decision affect me?" Christ invites us to ask a different question: "How will this decision uplift the needy?" Answering this question requires us to account for the fact that only the government can do certain things, of which restraining the broadly exploitative practices of large corporations and providing an adequate social safety net are just a few. But even if the government were to accomplish these things, it would not reduce our personal and communal responsibility. When we see others exploited and know we can stem it, we must do so.

But we ought not get too confident in our political ability. As much as the state has the resources to alleviate poverty, our hope doesn't ultimately reside in it. The state and systems that perpetuate racial capitalism have something in common: they do not and cannot ultimately operate by the logic of the kingdom of God. Only the church can do that. This means that the systems within which we find ourselves will need reform as long as they are made up of sinful human beings. All political "victories" for the good of the poor are temporary, fleeting, and complicated. Our hope cannot be in any political state of affairs. Rather, we must remain firmly rooted in the knowledge that the Son of God will return and set all things right. In the meantime, we do what we can with what we have. But doing what we can must begin with doing away with greed and exploitation wherever we find them.

Money's Hidden Fist

The deepest problem with exploitation is not that it is unfair but that it kills. Economic deprivation often leads to death, which means that it is fundamentally violent. That violence is necessary to keep the system running. As political commentator

Thomas Friedman said in 1999 about the globalizing economy, "The hidden hand of the market will never work without a hidden fist. . . . And the hidden fist that keeps the world safe . . . is called the United States Army, Air Force, Navy and Marine Corps."[9] For Friedman, the United States is a benign superpower, wielding its military might for good. For the Christian, however, the words *benign* and *military might* belong nowhere near one another. The Christian life has no place for the fist, especially the fist that is raised to exploit.

Subtly, it is that point that also challenges the specter of Marxism: Is the only way to enact this political economy through violent revolution? By no means! In fact, the use of violence runs counter to the kingdom of God. At the core of the Christian ethic is not only material solidarity and sharing but also an abhorrence of death and a commitment to the life of our neighbors. As the Westminster Larger Catechism states, the sixth commandment, "You shall not murder," includes "all careful studies, and lawful endeavors, to preserve the life of ourselves and others by resisting all thoughts and purposes, subduing all passions, and avoiding all occasions, temptations, and practices, which tend to the unjust taking away the life of any."[10] The refusal to murder is paired with a commitment to protect ourselves and others physically and mentally. Where our thoughts, emotions, and actions incline us to rage and murder, we fight them. But it is not enough just to avoid murdering our neighbors. We must love them.

6

Love or Violence?

Christian nonviolence is not based on an ethic of respect
for life or on the tactical superiority of nonviolence, but
on the determination to confront evil at its very root.

—Antonio Gonzalez, *God's Reign
and the End of Empires*

To resist violence that enforces taking advantage of
our neighbors, we are called to creative anti-violence,
looking to seek our neighbors' good, flourishing, and
prosperity. It is not enough to stop killing our neighbors. We
must think creatively about how to enhance each other's lives.

Violence continues to be the least creative way to respond to
violence. Instead, the New Testament and the early Christian
communities demonstrate that Christ has called each of us to
both avoid violence and actively quell it. Christians and their
communities must array themselves against both the quick killing of violent wrath and war and the slower killing of other
kinds of violence, like poverty and hunger.

Recall Francis Grimké's responses to lynching. He rightly
saw domination and social control as the purposes of lynching

and racial violence more broadly, but he argued that domination could only be out-dominated. In other words, fight violence with violence. But this is an argument of desperation rather than one of principle. We are not called to retaliate. We are called to make peace—in every circumstance we are able. Violence is an *enemy*, never a friend.

This is the peacemaking of the Beatitudes and the context in which we are to understand the nonresistance that Jesus teaches: not merely nonviolence but *anti-violence*. Put differently, the orientation of the Christian is *against violence*. Call it pacifism if you like, but most will associate pacifism with passivity or, even worse, failing to protect vulnerable people and accepting evil. The term *nonviolence* has similar connotations, even though Martin Luther King Jr. was very clear in advocating for nonviolent *resistance*. I prefer the language of *anti-violence*: it reminds us that we are indeed in a battle and that nonaction is not an option. But fighting fire with fire is not an option either. Why? Because no human being is our enemy such that we should kill them. Our enemies are not our fellow humans but the powers and principalities that seek to use us against one another.

The historical example of violence used throughout this book is lynching, a profoundly brutal instantiation of white supremacy. At the least, we ought to recoil at this form of subjugation. But many of us have grown cold to the numerous manifestations of violence that economic exploitation and political domination require: homelessness, poverty, hunger, thirst, and war. All of these are profoundly violent realities. Just as the hoarding of money is an example of this type of violence, so is the hoarding of opportunity.

Now, you might be thinking that this claim implies that everything is violent and that if everything is violent, then nothing is violent. True enough. Violence as considered here is anything that leads to death. Thus, our understanding of violence must stretch beyond murder but not so far as to include anything that leads to discomfort. When someone is kept from the material resources that are necessary for life, they are facing violence, and our responsibility in this scenario can be summed up in one word: *love*.

The Basis for Anti-Violence: What Is Love?

What is love? The Scriptures are the best place to look for a definition. Love is the central element of the two Great Commandments given to us by the Lord in the Old and New Testaments: to love the Lord our God with all our heart, soul, and strength and to love our neighbors as ourselves. These commands can appear nebulous. After all, what does it look like for me to love God, whom I cannot see? Who is my neighbor? Does loving someone mean that I have to feel warm and fuzzy about them? Thankfully, James, John, and Jesus have answers for us. For each of them, love is best understood fundamentally and inextricably as *material investment in one's neighbor*. You could probably guess that I would define love this way, given my earlier foregrounding of economic solidarity, but this definition goes beyond our use of money and possessions.

First John 3:11–18 provides a definition of *love* that answers our questions and also equips us to resist the talons of racialized capitalism. John begins with "the message you heard from the beginning: We should love one another" (v. 11) before moving to the paradigmatic opposite of love: murder. Following his Savior, John argues that *hate* and *murder* are synonymous and that the kingdom of God has no space for murder.[1] In fact, the consistent witness of the New Testament is against violence *in every way*. The nature of that connection, however, is not merely an emotional one. It is also a material one. Love is best expressed materially and so is its opposite. *Hate* and *killing* are synonymous in the ethical imagination of John precisely because snuffing out someone's life by one's own volition is the opposite of love.

If murder is a foil, however, what does John uphold as a positive example of love? The obvious answer is Christ, but a more specific answer is Christ considered *in his death*. John tells us clearly, "This is how we know what love is: Jesus Christ laid down his life for us. And we ought to lay down our lives for our brothers and sisters" (1 John 3:16). In case your imagination runs wild with that statement, assuming that one should just jump in front of bullets left and right, John then gives a specific example: "If anyone has material possessions and sees a brother or sister in need but has no pity on them, how can the love of God be in that person?" (3:17). James speaks in the same tenor: "Suppose a brother or a sister is without clothes and daily food. If one of you says to them, 'Go in peace; keep warm and well fed,' but does nothing about their physical needs, what good is it?" (James 2:15–16).

What actions determine whether one loves one's neighbor, one's brother or sister? According to James and John, love is always found in the provision of material possessions. In fact, the acts of salvation wrought by the Lord on our behalf, the clearest examples of God's love for his people, are inextricably material throughout the Scriptures. Whether we consider the exodus, the incarnation, the resurrection, or the final return of Christ, we are considering a bodily reality: the liberation from physical and economic oppression; the quite literal enfleshment of God; the defeat of death exemplified in Christ's new resurrected body, a body that cannot die again; and the final reign of the kingdom of God, complete with a new heaven and a new earth. The Scriptures drive deep into our minds the materiality not only of our existence but also of our love.

Jesus presses the issue of materiality throughout his life and teaching, but he does so especially in the Sermon on the Mount. His relentless preaching against greed is the best example of this; he urges us to distribute our resources justly. For Jesus, this material commitment is not restricted to our neighbors, brothers, and sisters. Instead, it extends even to one's enemies. In fact, enemy love lies at the center of what distinguishes the Christian from the rest of the world! Remember Christ's words:

> I tell you, love your enemies and pray for those who persecute you, that you may be children of your Father in heaven. He causes his sun to rise on the evil and the good, and sends rain on the righteous and the unrighteous. If you love those who love you, what reward will you get? Are not even the tax collectors doing that? And if you greet only your own people, what are you doing more than others? Do not even pagans do that? Be perfect, therefore, as your heavenly Father is perfect. (Matt. 5:44–48)

Every excuse to kill that sounds reasonable is a call to kill one's enemy, whether one's personal enemy or one's political enemy. It is even the reason for lethal self-defense: If you don't kill your attacker, what other options do you have? In the heat of being attacked, you will rely on your instincts. And if your instincts have not been formed by the gospel, they will tend away from Christ's commands. Every "but" is met with Jesus's framing of the Father, who gives life to both the evil and the good. If we are to be children of this same Father, we are to live in accord with that divine model. That is perfection.

By making these claims, I recognize the uphill battle that lies before me. The voice of Malcolm X, the man after whom I was named, rings in my head, telling me that the most effective way to battle violence is to recognize my own dignity and speak in a language that violence understands. In the context of racial justice, Malcolm's claims make so much sense. When someone raises their hand against you with murderous intent, it seems that the affirmation of your dignity should manifest itself in the violent protection of your life. Yet Jesus's voice rings out:

"If anyone slaps you on the right cheek, turn to them the other cheek also" (Matt. 5:39).

So, then, how should we define *love*? I like to view love as an economy, even a political economy. It is about the use and distribution of power and resources. Love, as Christ has revealed it to us, has to do primarily with our management, production, and exchange of resources, material and spiritual. This is not the most appealing or convenient way to conceive of love, but it is a particularly powerful witness of the church. When everything we possess is a gift from a loving God, love looks like sharing.

Anti-Violence Proper

Remember: the second arm of the demonic cycle of self-interest is violence. It is a necessary arm, as it is the arm that wields the sword. Once the believer has been united to Christ, however, the sword of steel has been removed from their hands. The sword of the Spirit replaces it. As Tertullian said at the turn of the third century, "Although soldiers had approached John [the Baptist] to receive instructions and a centurion believed, this does not change the fact that afterward, the Lord, by disarming Peter, disarmed every soldier."[2] We should never kill each other, and as far as we are able, we should not contribute to one another's deaths. The Christian is called to consistent anti-violence in their personal, social, and political life. To hold such a position is to conform to the commands of Christ and the Scriptures as a whole. God always intended his people to be a people who do not kill but rather depend on the Lord for their protection. This is a much harder position to hold than one of self-protection, yet it is the position that the people of God were expected to hold to in the face of warring nations. To see this, we have to take seriously three biblical texts: 1 Samuel 8, Matthew 5:38–48, and Romans 12:9–21.

118

A Great Tragedy: 1 Samuel 8

Besides the fall of Adam and Eve, the events of 1 Samuel 8 relay the greatest tragedy of the Old Testament. The people of God sacrifice their intimacy with God, their calling to be an alternative among the nations, and many of their supposed egalitarian freedoms for one request: a human king.

Israel desires to be like the other nations, so the elders approach Samuel with this request. After consulting with the Lord, Samuel tells them all the things a king will do to them. The first thing Samuel tells them is that the king "will take your sons and appoint them to his chariots and to be his horsemen and to run before his chariots. And he will appoint for himself commanders of thousands and commanders of fifties, and some to plow his ground and to reap his harvest, and to make his implements of war and the equipment of his chariots" (1 Sam. 8:11 ESV). The king will build and grow a military, tax the people extensively, and ultimately enslave them. He will live by the logic of violence, using it to secure and defend land. And he will exploit his people for personal gain. This is precisely what happened in the history of the monarchy.

This tragic reality undermines Israel's founding identity. Theologian Antonio González draws our attention back to the song that Moses and the Israelites sing after their deliverance, especially the words of Exodus 15:18: "The LORD reigns for ever and ever!" As opposed to Pharoah's exploitative reign, the Israelites are supposed to live, from the perspective of this song, as "a people governed by God."[3] They are supposed to remain faithful to the Lord, who will provide everything they need to live: land, food, work, and all other necessities. Problems arise when they reach out their hands to obtain those things for themselves, the same error made by Adam and Eve.

The request for a monarch is, then, more than just a political error. It is a theological one. It is the people of God telling

God, "We want the good things of the world by the world's means." Also: "We see our fellow nations with armies to fight for them. We want some of that too." Instead of depending on the Lord, they want to defend themselves. The remainder of the Old Testament outlines the outcome of such a choice: oppression of the poor, both from within and from without; idolatry; war; and exile. How fitting that Isaiah's vision of the future addresses these elements of their existence head on! In the second chapter of his prophetic book, Isaiah describes the mountain of the Lord, the redeemed location of God's people, with these words: "[The LORD] will judge between the nations and will settle disputes for many peoples. They will beat their swords into plowshares and their spears into pruning hooks. Nation will not take up sword against nation, nor will they train for war anymore. Come, descendants of Jacob, let us walk in the light of the LORD" (Isa. 2:4–5).

Walking in this light means living as a people over whom God reigns. At the least, it means living as a people who do not train for war and whose instruments of death have been turned into tools for feeding.

Against Old-Time Religion: Matthew 5:38–48

First Samuel gives an abstract foundation; Jesus's own explicit words give concrete examples. Primarily, the people of God are called to lead lives of creative anti-violence because Jesus tells us to live in such a way. Insofar as Christ mirrors Moses's role on Mount Sinai in his Sermon on the Mount, he offers the people of God a new charter of conduct, a robust picture of what it means to be a community ruled by God. Unlike Moses, Christ gives his commands knowing that he is also giving his people the resources to obey them. When the Holy Spirit descends on them and dwells within them, they can actually be the community that God has called them to be.

That community is a nonviolent one, exemplified in Christ's words about revenge and how we are to treat our enemies. The Sermon on the Mount is saturated with this call. The Beatitudes define meekness and gentleness as necessities. Jesus tells us that the meek will inherit the earth, refuting the common and colonial wisdom that the land goes to those who wrest it violently from the clutches of those who need it. Even just this beatitude cuts against much of the history of lynching: as a violent expression of white supremacy and greed, racial violence is antithetical to the gospel. The talons of racial capitalism communicate to the world that might makes right, while Christ continually presses the way of nonviolence. He makes this point most explicitly, however, in Matthew 5:38–48—his back-to-back condemnations of both the lex talionis, the common law of revenge, and a preferential love for one's friends and a corresponding hate for one's enemies. If we seek to be people united to this Savior, we must do what he says!

For some of us, though, the words of Malcolm X ring louder in our ears than the words of Jesus. In his "Message to the Grassroots," Malcolm reminds his hearers of what they have in common: being persecuted and exploited by racist white people. He pulls no punches in describing the harms suffered and the solidarity that flow from an affirmation of Black identity; after all, "you catch hell 'cause you're a black man. You catch hell, all of us catch hell, for the same reason."[4] The white man is the enemy, and what do you do when the enemy comes at you? You put them down!

Malcolm's logic seems airtight. In a sequence in his speech, he argues that "if violence is wrong in America, violence is wrong abroad."[5] In other words, if defending Black people violently is wrong, as some argue, then defending the country violently in war is also wrong. Conversely, if drafting is all right, so is self-defense! In that sequence, Malcolm banks on an audience that sees no broader issue with the violence of war and applies that logic to a violent American milieu, where Black men, women, and children are subjected to similar, warlike conditions. For Malcolm, especially early Malcolm, revolution is always bloody because defending oneself demands it. He also knows, however, that he has contemporaries who insist on nonviolence. So he aims squarely at them and their religious claims in the middle of his speech:

> There is nothing in our book, the Quran—you call it "Koran"—that teaches us to suffer peacefully. Our religion teaches us to be intelligent. Be peaceful, be courteous, obey the law, respect everyone, but if someone puts his hand on you, send him to the cemetery. That's a good religion. In fact, that's that old-time religion. That's the one that Ma and Pa used to talk about: an eye for an eye, and a tooth for a tooth, and a head for a head, and a life for a life. That's a good religion. And doesn't nobody resent that kind of religion being taught but a wolf, who intends to make you his meal.[6]

Malcolm argues that a religion of nonviolence is a religion of stupidity, vulnerability, and weakness, *especially for Black people*. It's unintelligent to think that your enemy will relent if you don't respond in kind. Not only that, such thinking places you at great risk and could ultimately lead to your death! Because Afro-Americans have faced the most egregious kinds of violence, it's all the more reasonable for us to respond as Malcolm argues we should. But while such a response may be reasonable, it is not righteous.

Jesus doesn't mince words about the logic of retaliation and revenge. Christians are called to consider their lives and the situations in which they might be tempted to seek revenge and refuse to do so. Chances are the specific situations in Matthew 5:38–42 don't actually apply to you. People may not be slapping you in the face, suing you for your shirt, or forcing you to walk a mile. But each of us can remember times when others have harmed us or sought to harm us. In most of those cases, our first impulse may have been to lash out, at the very least to ensure that the offender gets a taste of their own medicine. If we cannot stomach one thing, it is someone *getting away with evil*. Yet when we retaliate, we are refusing to do the hardest and most essential action we are called by Christ to do, which is to forgive. In fact, the refusal to respond to evil with evil is what the kingdom of God is about! We aim at the very heart of sin by being a community that lives in the way of forgiveness and shows the world that the kingdom of God is real.

In case you think Jesus is joking about nonretaliation and has somehow forgotten about the fact that people might want to kill you, he follows up the command not to retaliate against an evil person with the command to specifically care for one's enemies. His reasoning is fascinating: we are to love our enemies so that we "may be children of [our] Father in heaven" (Matt. 5:45). The sunrise and rainfall benefit everyone, whether righteous or wicked, and Christ is telling us, relatedly, to use our resources for everyone's flourishing. Lest the reader think this is just a secondary ethical command, Christ summarizes it bracingly: "Be perfect, therefore, as your heavenly Father is perfect" (5:48). Whether you understand the Greek *teleios* to mean "perfect," "whole," or "complete," the point is clear: we are called to be like God, precisely in his generosity to those who hate him.

Most of all, however, the picture of nonretaliation and enemy love is exemplified in the life of Jesus, depicted throughout the Gospels. The One who has most reason to lash out against his enemies refuses to do so. He doesn't just live that way as a kind of unattainable model. He lives that way precisely to offer a model *attainable* by the same power with which he does those things: the power of the Holy Spirit. Is it hard to forgive, to eat a cost, to not strike back when we are struck? Of course! But none of that has any bearing on whether or not Christ has told us to do so. And he has. This takes violence off the table for the Christian.

We are called to imagine and build, within Christian community, the world that Christ has born witness to in his words and his life. As our Savior refuses to retaliate, so must we. As our Savior extends grace not only to his friends but also to those who have betrayed and sought to kill him, so also must we. Jesus feeds and washes the feet of Judas. That is the logic of the gospel and the picture of love: material care for all who need it.

But What about the State? Romans 12 and 13

Some hearing my disavowal of all violence and my encouragement that no Christian engage in it will immediately think of Romans 13. This is understandable. Romans 13 has to be understood within the context of Romans 12, a text that sounds very much like Jesus does in the Sermon on the Mount.

Near the end of most Protestants' favorite New Testament epistle are three chapters of sustained application of the gospel, Romans 12–14. But Paul begins these chapters by focusing on the material: calling us to offer our bodies as a living sacrifice, Paul by the Spirit reminds us that we love with our bodies, not merely with our minds. Our faith is a material, bodily faith: a faith in which we offer our flesh, our hands, our feet, and all that we possess to God's service. After all, Christ offered all for us! In order to do so, however, we have to heed Paul's words in Romans 12:2—namely, that we do not conform to the world but instead are transformed by the Spirit. Our example is different from that of the world because our example is the incarnate and resurrected Lord in all things, without exception. That must include our view of revenge and violence; Paul, like his Lord, agrees.

Romans 12:9–21 is essentially Paul's definition of *love*. A community saturated with Christian love is a community of joy and patience (v. 12). It is characterized by material sharing (v. 13). But it is also a community that responds to evil in a specific way. Echoing Jesus, Paul reminds us to bless those who persecute us and never to fight evil with evil. Like the Savior, he is relentless on this theme and brings it home in verses 19–20, where he quotes Deuteronomy 32:35 and Proverbs 25:21–22: "Do not take revenge, my dear friends, but leave room for God's wrath, for it is written: 'It is mine to avenge; I will repay,' says the Lord. On the contrary: 'If your enemy is hungry, feed him; if he is thirsty, give him something to drink. In doing this, you will heap burning coals on his head.'"

Paul adds an element to the Christian refusal of revenge and a reason that Jesus does not include in the Sermon on the Mount: divine wrath. He reminds us that God's judgment is more comprehensive, wiser, and more just than ours, so we should leave it to him. Christ focuses on modeling the love of the Father, but Paul gives us another component: God hates evil more than we do, and he takes it personally. The question is whether we trust him to handle it. Refusing violence and revenge doesn't diminish evil. It rather recognizes that responding to evil with evil is inadequate. Instead, as Paul puts it, we are in all things to overcome evil with good.

Paul then proceeds to a *contrasting* institution, an institution that operates by a different logic than the kingdom does. The Christian's political theology is summed up in this statement: the most effective way to effect social change is to form an alternative society. When we say that Christ is the only way to salvation, we ought not mean only that our souls find rest in Christ—though that is true! What is bound up in that claim is that the most truly human, most truly joyful, and most truly abundant life is a life lived in union with Christ and with his people, living according to the logic of his kingdom. If this is true and if our actions and imaginations have been shaped accordingly, then Romans 13:1–7 is revealed for what it is: guidance for how

Christians address a system outside themselves. How else could we, after being told that we must overcome our enemies by feeding them, respond to an institution that wields the sword against evildoers? The principles at the root of the two institutions are wildly different: at the root of the church is neighbor love, whereas at the root of the state is most often imperial and retributive violence aimed at accumulation.

If this is true, then González is also right in saying that when Paul describes this contradiction, "he can hardly be thinking that Christians should participate in imperial power."[7] Christians may look to Joseph, Esther, and Daniel as models for Christian involvement in the state, but none of them actually changes their state. In fact, each actually participates in the violent logic of the state.[8] Esther is restricted by such logic as a victim of sex trafficking. Joseph enacts it in Genesis 47, as he is the one who, after taking the Egyptians' and Canaanites' money and livestock, ultimately places them in a position where all they have is their bodies and their land. Daniel, while a faithful presence in the Babylonian Empire, cannot stop Babylon from being Babylon. The very same lions that do not devour him devour others, including those who falsely accuse him and their families. Empires kill. But Christians cannot.

In this sense, both the Christian nationalist and the progressive Christian bent on political power are wrong. Both sides argue that the journey to salvation includes a road to political power, although the former has done so with more explicit violence. We are told that if we just get more Christians into positions of political power, the world will change. But that logic remains coercive: the change that we would be initiating in those spaces would be forced. For both sides, victory looks like domination rather than invitation, no matter how apparently benign that domination is. To the contrary, the Christian's relationship with the government is to be one of submission, provided they are not commanded to violate the law of God.

So practically, what does all of this mean for the church? How can the church be an anti-violent community amid a violent world? Such a question lies at the core of our ethical witness. To these practicalities we now turn.

What Is the Anti-Violent Church? Preaching, Practices, and Politics

At its root, the Christian commitment to anti-violence is a commitment to root out and eliminate violence, especially in our midst. We will get irredeemably frustrated if we think we can eradicate violence in the world at large, and anyone who understands the systemic nature of race and racial violence feels that frustration regularly. But the Christian ethic of love demands that we seek to eradicate violence everywhere we are, including the spaces that can operate by the logic of the kingdom of God. These redeemable spaces are threefold: the self, the family, and the church. An anti-violent ethic, if we are to see it, must be visible in these three spaces before it is visible anywhere else.

Resistance to violence, like resistance to greed, should manifest in our preaching, our practices, and our politics. The Scriptures call us to be personal, communal, and cosmic peacemakers in union with the Prince of Peace. The people of God need to be encouraged regularly to live in such a way, to pursue peace in their families, in their communities, and in their churches. True peace is the active presence of love and justice, not merely the absence of violence. Our moral imaginations are to be shaped more by the Scriptures than by political "common sense." Whereas some refer to the right to defend themselves, the Christian must refer to the command to love others. Such love requires that we root out harshness and violence from our relationships with our families, brothers, sisters, and neighbors and instead exalt the third beatitude:

127

"Blessed are the meek, for they will inherit the earth" (Matt. 5:5).

When it comes to our practices and politics, an anti-violent ethic will manifest itself in the church as a resistance to, at the very least, the two most prominent examples of violence in the world: poverty and war. The forms of violence that surround us daily are often handmaidens and symptoms of poverty, but the self, the family, and the church can immediately address two of them: hunger and lack of adequate, affordable housing. I choose these two particularly because in the Scriptures food and shelter are presented as necessary ingredients in human contentment and two items that Christians are to provide for their needy neighbors. The material definitions of *love* pressed by Jesus, James, John, and Paul all center on making sure that others have food, clothing, and shelter and that they are warm and nourished. Yet even though racial capitalism and its attendant systems use hunger and homelessness to kill slowly, communities and individuals can mobilize to beat them back.

What this looks like will depend on your city and community. But everyone needs somewhere to start. It can begin with your family folding members of your community into your dinner meals. It can begin with building relationships with the food banks in your area. But it can also mean attending to the ways hunger and housing are racialized. For example, Junia Howell has underscored that housing appraisals are deeply racialized, and it is not the fault of the appraisers.[9] Rather, the problem resides in the very equations used to calculate home values. Housing, in many of our minds, is a source of profit and wealth rather than a resource for meeting the human need for shelter (its primary purpose). The words of Isaiah aim at any of us who seek to build wealth through amassing property: "Woe to you who add house to house and join field to field till no space is left and you live alone in the land!" (Isa. 5:8). What if we viewed our homes not merely as enclaves for our families but as sites of hospitality? What if we viewed housing and clothing as resources that everyone needs and advocated accordingly? Our practices and politics ought to reflect such commitments. The most practical way to resist violence is to feed, clothe, and house our neighbors, friends, and enemies.

Opposition to war is, while controversial, rather self-explanatory. The New Testament teaches that the Christian ought to have no part in it. As citizens of an often warmongering nation, we are called to bear witness to a different logic, just as the early church did in the face of Roman oppression: not one of boundary and border making but one of solidarity. Anti-violence is a fundamentally active stance. When people are framed as our enemies, we must insist that they are fed and clothed, not killed. The church in its first few centuries knew this to be true and lived accordingly, exposing themselves to the wrath of a state that demanded total allegiance. That threat did not faze them. The final beatitude looms over the Christian life: "Blessed are those who are persecuted because of righteousness, for theirs is the kingdom of heaven" (Matt. 5:10). If we are persecuted, at least let it be for doing what Christ has commanded us to do.

But some of you will remain unconvinced about my treatment of war. After all, isn't just war an exception? It has been for much of Christian history, but just because a belief is common, even for a vast majority of Christians, does not mean that it is Christlike. Sometimes, Christian communities believe and advocate for particular positions because they are more politically convenient. Just war is precisely one of those positions.

But What about . . . ? The Historic Christian Tradition

If one line of moral inquiry incites many to ask about exceptions, it is that of lethal violence. Are we ever to engage in such violence? Given the tremendous stakes of the battle against racial capitalism, surely we cannot take an option off the table, can we? The ire that a public, conceptual resistance to war and violence inspires should give us pause: Why are we so eager to find exceptions to anti-violence and so resistant to eschewing violence? We can ask something similar about our greed: Why are we so eager to hoard and so reticent to share? Martin Luther King Jr. was killed soon after his ministry took a more explicitly anti-war and anti-poverty stance. This is not coincidental: he began to strike at the very heart of the racial-capitalist system—and the talons struck him. We expose ourselves to the same risk when we aim at the system's heart rather than its extremities. So Christians' unqualified resistance to lethal violence is bound to raise some hackles. After all, we're used to making exceptions.

Much of the Christian tradition has made such exceptions, including the Westminster Catechism. After outlining the duties of the sixth commandment, including the commitment to materially support and love one's neighbor, the divines outline the particular sins forbidden by the sixth commandment and give three examples of permissible lethal violence: "public justice, lawful war, and necessary defense."[10] In other words, you're allowed to kill by means of the state (think: the criminal justice system or war) and in self-defense. One could very easily justify mounting a war against an exploitative political economy by means of state power or under the auspices of self-defense. Notably, however, the Scriptures cited in support of these exceptions are all from the Old Testament. The divines draw from Numbers, Jeremiah, Deuteronomy, and Exodus to justify a pretty serious claim—that killing is still admissible for the Christian. In fact, the only point at which the Sermon on the Mount appears in the Scripture proofs for Westminster's explanation is when Jesus's words on anger and worry are referenced (see Matt. 5:22 on sinful anger and Matt. 6:31, 34 on distracting cares). These words, however, are not Christ's strongest against murder. His words against vengeance take that title. When Christ called us to love our enemies, to pray for those who persecute us, and not to resist an evil person in kind, he disarmed us. The reasoning for lethal violence in self-defense is uncomfortably hamstrung by Christ's own words.

Also, historical context is important. As New Testament scholar Richard Hays has noted, "Although the tradition of the first three centuries was decidedly pacifist in orientation, Christian tradition from the time of Constantine to the present has predominantly endorsed war, or at least justified it under certain conditions."[11] As Hays argues, the criteria for just war have been dictated more by natural law traditions than by the Scriptures. On the other hand, "the New Testament offers no basis for ever declaring Christian participation in war 'just.'"[12] One of the reasons why the Christian tradition has argued for just war theory, however, is that it puts the church in a less risky political position. It is much more attractive to affirm the violence of a state that is sympathetic to your interests than to resist it. Such was the case with Augustine in the early fifth century and the Westminster Assembly in the seventeenth century.

The writers of the Westminster Standards vied for both ecclesiastical unity and political authority. When they gathered as an assembly (1643–49) to solidify the doctrine of seventeenth-century Presbyterianism, they did so hoping to rule England. For them, a healthy marriage between church and state was ideal. That historical fact shaped their theological positions. For example, the confession that they wrote affirms that the magistrate, or government, cannot administer the sacraments but can suppress heresy, blasphemy, and corruption in worship. They had a magistrate much like the Old Testament monarchy. But the people of God were never meant to have a monarchy. Why build a robust Christian model around a political structure that God has wanted his people to avoid? The answer is simple: social location. When you are in power, you want to stay in power. The logic of James and John asking Jesus for right and left seats is the same logic that tells Christians to use the power of the state for the so-called gospel. That logic refuses to acknowledge that Christ's kingdom is not of this world. To say that the kingdom of God is not "of this world" is to say that it is otherworldly not in application but rather in origin. Few things are more this-worldly than ambition, domination, and violence. For the Westminster Assembly, theology flowed from social temptations.

Two other English confessional bodies understood the government differently. The Independents, a minority, affirmed in their confessional document, the Savoy Declaration, that the magistrate was meant to "encourage, promote, and protect" the church.[13] But the Baptists articulated the role of the government without reference to the church at all. As a persecuted body, they had no hope of political power nor any desire to conceive of a world in which church and state were married, however tenuous that union might be. Instead, the Baptists appealed to the words of the New Testament, affirming that Christians are to pray for their rulers and pray "that under them we may live a quiet and peaceable life, in all godliness and honesty."[14] They never referenced the government protecting or enforcing anything for the sake of the church because the persecuted are those who most know the devastation of power misused. All they wanted was space for the church to continue to be the church.

Why look so closely at old English confessions? Because they remind us that social location matters in theological formation. Positions of power can often keep us from heeding the words of Christ. Christ's commands compel us, regardless of the state's sympathies or hostilities toward us. As a matter of fact, if the church occupies its proper role, the final beatitude will be a proper description of our lives: "Blessed are those who are persecuted because of righteousness, for theirs is the kingdom of heaven. Blessed are you when people insult you, persecute you and falsely say all kinds of evil against you because of me.

Rejoice and be glad, because great is your reward in heaven, for in the same way they persecuted the prophets who were before you" (Matt. 5:10–12).

We ought to heed the persecuted more than the powerful. After all, Jesus sides with the former and opposes the latter, reminding us that his kingdom is not of this world. The logic of the kingdom of God does not allow for the use of coercive violence.

Because that is the case, instead of heeding the Westminster divines, we should heed the historic Christian peace traditions on this point. As an example, the Mennonite Church USA's confession of faith exhibits these powerful words on violence: "As followers of Jesus, we participate in his ministry of peace and justice. . . . The same Spirit that empowered Jesus also empowers us to love enemies, to forgive rather than to seek revenge, to practice right relationships, to rely on the community of faith to settle disputes, and to resist evil without violence. Led by the Spirit, and beginning in the church, we witness to all people that violence is not the will of God."[15]

No exceptions here. When Jesus says to love our enemies and to feed them, he does not distinguish them by nation, race, or any other category. He says that even our enemy is our neighbor, and the Great Commandment is to love them. Even when we are faced with a phenomenon as brutal as lynching or as pervasive as the racial-capitalist cycle, the Christian's response cannot be dictated or diluted by their circumstances. Instead, union with Christ must be the controlling perspective, looking to the Savior as both redeemer and exemplar.

But What about . . . ? Liberation Theology

The position outlined above is unpopular, especially within mainstream Christian circles. But it can be especially unattractive to those who witness injustice most palpably. Amid tragedy and injustice, it is easy, out of desperation, to fight them by any means necessary. Some argue that when racial violence and oppression are in view, the oppressed must respond or, at least, are justified in responding with self-defense. Here, I think of the powerful voices of Black liberation theology, especially that of James Cone.

The question is this: Is Cone right? Does the prohibition of lethal violence have any exceptions?

No theologian has been more familiar with the depths of racial violence than the great theologian of the cross and the lynching tree. As an element of his earlier liberation theology, Cone had to ask and answer the question of the role of violence in liberatory struggle. Near the end of *Black Theology and Black Power*, he asks the question squarely, recognizing that if we are to speak of revolution, we have to ask about violence. Cone looks with clear eyes on the single most important obstacle to revolutionary violence, writing that "our chief difficulty with Black Theology and violence, however, arises from the New Testament itself."[16] Jesus is never violent and never condones violence. Cone sidesteps this barrier, arguing that to see Christ as an example in this regard is to become subject to a rigid fundamentalism and literalism. We do not face the same choices as Jesus did, Cone tells us. After all, he was in the first century, and we are in the twenty-first century. In that sense, Jesus's own choices are irrelevant to our moral reasoning. Cone proceeds by relativizing the entire set of questions, following one of the founders of Latin American liberation theology, José Miguez Bonino. Because the world is a world of violence, a true nonviolent option doesn't exist: "It is this fact that most whites seem to overlook—the fact that violence already exists. The Christian does not decide between violence and nonviolence, evil and good. He decides between the less and the greater evil. He must ponder whether revolutionary violence is less or more deplorable than the violence perpetuated by the system."[17]

Cone thought it impossible to keep one's hands clean of violence. In a system so saturated with violence and the logic of violence, the Christian has a choice: side with revolutionary violence or side with systemic violence. So-called nonviolence sides with the latter, at least in an American context.

Cone would revisit the issue in *God of the Oppressed* because any theology that attempts to truly reckon with race must reckon with violence. Cone saves his assessment of violence for the end of his book. At the forefront of his mind is whether oppressed Black people can justly lash out at their white oppressors with violence. He concludes: don't let "white rhetoric about nonviolence and Jesus" cloud your mind.[18] For Cone, white people appeal to the nonviolence of Jesus to get Black people to docilely accept their subjugation. Such a move is a move of utmost hypocrisy, as white people, through the construction of race and throughout the history of the United States, have used violence to create a society in which Black people have been regularly oppressed and exploited. He repeats his argument, that it is impossible to be nonviolent in a violent, oppressive, and exploitative world. He also deepens his argument about the role of Jesus in the New Testament, saying that the Christian's foremost concern is not what Jesus did but what Jesus is doing, and the only way to discern the current work of Jesus is to behold the struggles of the oppressed. White theologians, Cone argues, will do what they can to push those struggles aside. They are concerned only about using Christ's nonviolence to quash any attempts to resist the status quo. If anyone is to set the agenda, for Cone, it has to be the oppressed.[19]

Cone's points are powerful and compelling but ultimately unpersuasive. Thankfully, the moral universe offers more choices than just capitulating to systemic violence. Early on Cone seems to have submitted to tragedy; profound violence and exploitation can do that to a person. We've seen it happen with Francis Grimké, who began to see violent self-defense, later in life, as the only way to curb lynching. Cone's framing of our moral and ethical options is constrained by the fact that he thinks about the Christian, at least with respect to violence, as an individual, whereas we must consider ourselves as *communities*. That is, what kinds of actions are we going to encourage one another to pursue? The call of Christ is to do something new by the power of the Spirit. It is not to succumb to thinking that we must choose among only evil options. It is to follow a Spirit-filled imagination and consider whether we can create good options. It is to flee from the logic that dictates violence as the only option and to ask the Lord, What does it mean to create a community of love, nonviolence, faith, and Christlikeness and to invite people into this community?

Ultimately, it's a grave mistake to dismiss Christ's particular actions and words as irrelevant today, especially on a topic as ubiquitous as violence. It is, of course, reprehensible for white theologians to use Christ in an effort to pacify those they unjustly exploit, but Christ's message has value even when it proceeds from unclean mouths. When Jesus speaks against the Pharisees, he encourages his disciples to do what they command, because their teaching is still rooted in the law of God, but he discourages his disciples from mimicking their actions. The same hypocritical dynamic is present here: white theologians who have used Christ's commands of nonviolence to ignore and justify and maintain their own violence are subject to the same judgment that Jesus reserves for the Pharisees and the teachers of the law. The Son of God took on flesh to destroy the works of the devil and to reveal both the character of God and the true shape of the human life. The life of Christ is a paradigmatic human life, relevant for every human being who has ever lived. Marvelously, this is precisely the way God chose to reveal himself to us: not in the sky but in a manger.

One of my favorite theologians, Cyril of Alexandria, describes the purpose of the incarnation as he reflects on Christ's final words on the cross: "It was necessary for us to have the beneficial knowledge of how far the limits of obedience should extend, by what wonderful ways it comes, how great is its reward, and what form it has."[20] The life that Christ lived is specifically for our benefit, especially as an example of what obedience looks like and what it yields. That even applies to violence: Christ, by his life, reveals that we are to be a people ever more ready to suffer than to kill. But the mystery grows even deeper: Christ also displays and teaches the ethic of the kingdom of God, an ethic that reflects God's own heart. Nonviolence or, as I have termed it, anti-violence, is a significant part of that ethic.

An anti-violence ethic is an ethic of suffering. It couldn't be any other way. Jesus isn't joking or exaggerating when he says that whoever wishes to be a disciple must take up their method of execution and walk in his footsteps (see Matt. 10:38; Luke 9:23). In his early theology, Cone resisted these conclusions, identifying them as weak in the face of overwhelming violence. Perhaps that is too harsh of a judgment. Cone, like many of us, probably deemed nonviolence impractical and ineffective. The life of Christ, however, shatters those strictures. After all, Jesus doesn't physically resist his oppressors. Instead, he chooses to die, inviting us all to do likewise. While such a choice doesn't sound like victory, the resurrection bears a different story. Raised from the dead, Christ is vindicated personally, and his method is as well. In order to be raised in union with Christ, we are called to live lives in union with him, patterned after his way of life. Cone resisted these conclusions in his early theology, but he would eventually recognize their worth. It took a deep dive into lynching to drive these truths into his soul.

After writing *The Cross and the Lynching Tree*, Cone was reminded of the only and most powerful way to resist suffering: to point oneself to the cross and to a community that gathers under the cross in solidarity. Whereas he resisted King's commitment to nonviolence decades beforehand, Cone came to recognize Christ's forgiveness as "spiritual resistance, a revolt against hatred, [and] the refusal to allow the hater to make you like him."[21] He saw that nonviolence was love, the most powerful way to resist violent white supremacy. In seeing Christ more clearly, Cone began to see the possibilities of a beloved community in which exploitation and violence are no more because the people of God love as Christ has called them to love, regardless of racial identity. It was ultimately the cross that drilled nonviolence (or anti-violence) into Cone's soul in the final year of his life; it is only the cross that will do the same in each and every one of us.

The Final Leg of the Cycle

We are encouraged to make exceptions to Christ's commands because we think he asks too much of us. It is far too difficult for me to think creatively about resisting violence when I can lash out at my aggressor. It is far too difficult for me to respond with grace and love when my enemy is insistent on treating me like garbage. But violence and retaliation are the least creative responses to evil. The body of Christ is called to holy creativity. Two of the ways that we communally battle the powers and principalities that lie behind the demonic cycle of self-interest are by resisting greed in communities of economic solidarity and by working a robust anti-violence into ourselves, our families, and our communities. But one more piece of the cycle remains. Economic exploitation and greed require violence, to be sure, but they also require lies, of which race is one. If we are the body of Christ living in union with him, sharing his priorities and serving as beacons of his love, then we must prophetically tell the truth.

7

Truth or Lies?

> The way to right wrongs is to turn the light of truth upon
> them.
>
> —Ida B. Wells, *The Light of Truth*

I f we were to personify racial capitalism, violence and exploitation would be its arms, reaching out to kill. We have
discussed some of the ways to disable those arms. But racial capitalism has legs too, the means by which it travels and
spreads. The history of race is the history of lies meant to
justify structures of exploitation. To resist the lies of racial
categorization and the smoke screen that race creates, we have
to build communities that relentlessly pry, relentlessly ask questions, and relentlessly proclaim the truth about ourselves and
those around us.

Ida B. Wells is our paradigmatic truth teller. She recognized
truth telling as one of her primary tasks; she knew in her soul
that the way to fight evil was to illuminate it fully. We cannot
fight what we do not see. We cannot fight racism well if we
think that it is just about power or hate or ignorance. To only
see and speak of those things is to operate with clouded sight

and bound hands and feet. We must see the other material element of race and racism: money. This truth is uncomfortable, but we will not rid ourselves of race and racism without loudly proclaiming it.

We are bombarded daily with justifications of the violence and exploitation that we witness, narratives that obscure the humanity of our neighbors. The gospel calls us to affirm a deeper truth and to refuse to allow hierarchies of power to separate us and prevent us from meeting each other's needs. If the powers and principalities that maintain systems of racialized exploitation and domination want us dead, we have to expend ourselves wisely, keeping one another alive as long as we can. In fact, this is what a life submitted to the lordship of Christ must do. It is not an option for the Christian; rather, it reflects a robust understanding of the commands of Christ, and it publicly displays what it means to be united to him.

Violence and exploitation distract us from the fact that, at its root, race is a lie that keeps us from seeing our neighbors as neighbors. Recall Christ's parable of the "good Samaritan," an already socially constructed title that draws attention to the ways in which ethnicity is used to divide. The parable is a master class in the reversal of expectations. It is Jesus's way of revealing the prejudices and obfuscations of an unnamed expert in the law who seeks to test him. The man asks, "Who is my neighbor?" Jesus responds with the parable and a different question: "Who acted as a neighbor?" The self-justifying person encounters the needy and asks, "Does this person deserve my love?" The Christ follower encounters the needy and asks, "How can I love this person?"

The fourth-century priest and bishop John Chrysostom says that other than need, no attributes determine whether someone "deserves" our loving care: "Need alone is the poor man's worthiness; if anyone at all ever comes to us with this recommendation, let us not meddle any further."[1] For some of us, these words challenge our desire for meticulous prudence. What about the undeserving poor? What about the people who've gotten themselves into the situations they're in? What about the people who don't work hard enough or who've made sinful decisions? Are we just supposed to pour ourselves out for them? Jesus and John answer those questions the same way: Yes. After all, that is precisely the way Christ has loved us.

Viewed in this light, the lie of race is a method of justification, allowing us to see one another in categories beyond those the Lord espouses. The only category that matters is that of *neighbor*. Yet ideologies of ascriptive difference are meant to create categories of *deserving* and *undeserving*. We must always remember the purpose of race: to create and maintain hierarchies of power and money. Race as we know it is a set of narratives that has been used to justify material circumstances; therefore, we have to resist it in both material *and* narrative ways. And the church should be one space where we're reminded that race doesn't determine our life or identity.

This truth is not color blindness in disguise. It is not a roundabout way of saying that race doesn't matter. Race does, in our world, matter. We need to be reminded, however, that race ought not matter and, in the end, will not matter in substantive, soul-sucking ways. In this world, such a reminder requires us to mimic the Old Testament prophetic tradition: we must be willing to speak and apply the Word of God even though we will be rejected by many who hear. Like that of the Old Testament prophets, our first concern is not the laying out of the future but a laying out of the way the Lord would have us act now. As Amos warns those who are at ease in Zion, so we must warn those who have made their fortunes on the backs of the exploited in our current political economy. As Hosea warns Israel of the consequences of its spiritual adultery, so we must name the ways that racial capitalism amounts to Mammon worship. As Micah and Isaiah look forward to a world where the people of God no longer prepare for war, so we are called to build communities that live in precisely that way. All of this is made possible by our union with the One who is Prophet, Priest, and King: Jesus Christ.

Prophetic truth telling means that we have to intentionally dismantle the most significant narratives about race that surround us. Even in Christian circles, we are often told that racial reconciliation is the answer to racism: if we think differently about each other and build different friendships, racism will be beaten back. It's time we tell the truth to one another: systemic issues are not solved through hanging out. They are solved by relationships of solidarity. The powers and principalities are defeated by holy action empowered by the Holy Spirit. Reconciliation suggests the reforging of relationship, previously broken. Because race is a category of obfuscation and oppression, *racial reconciliation* is an oxymoron: you cannot repair something that was never whole to begin with. We have to image a set of relationships guided by brotherhood, sisterhood, and neighborliness. We have to image new systems founded on these relationships. And such imaging can truly happen only by seeing, recognizing, and defanging racialized realities.

When we are told that we should fight systemic racism by diving deeper into the particulars of racial identity, we must have the moral imagination to zoom out and recognize that the goal is not just to avoid being racist. The goal is to drain race of its power. The goal is not merely to eradicate racial disparity, though that is, in some ways, a good, proximate goal. The goal is that no person is a victim of injustice. When particular groups are singled out for exploitation and domination, we are called to live in solidarity with them.

For example, the Scriptures call believers to align themselves with the poor, the widow, and the orphan. But the Christian does not stop with solidarity. The Christian walks alongside the poor as they seek what they need to survive and thrive. The

Christian walks alongside the widow and all those who are socially vulnerable to build communities of care. The Christian walks alongside the orphan and surrounds them with the love of the family of God. In a society shot through with racial capitalism, the Christian bears witness to the fact that no human being is defined by an economic system's valuation of them. The Christian extends the same grace and mercy they have received from God to everyone in need around them. Where racial lies create hierarchies of worthiness, the Christian refuses to fall into their trap. Knowing that all human beings are created in the image of God, the Christian treats every person in a way that fits that identity.

Prophetic truth telling is not reserved for church leaders or so-called mature Christians alone. It is present in the first workings of the Spirit because it is, at root, simple. The battle against greed and violence is pitched against powers and principalities that create ever more complex systems. The battle against lies is much simpler: tell the truth and shame the devil. You may be told that someone's housing circumstances dictate whether they are worthy of food, life, or work. Refuse that as a lie. You may be told that certain enemies deserve death. Refuse that as a lie. You may be told that some are responsible for being exploited, dominated, or otherwise sinned against. Refuse that as a lie. Repentance requires us to both turn away from sin and toward one another.

As we mature in our union with Christ, we learn deeper ways to do both of those things. But our maturity begins with truth telling. We must know the truth about ourselves—that we have been created for union with God. Sin is insistent on keeping us from that union, but the triune God is much more insistent that we experience it. Thus, we need to be clear about race's ongoing, insidious work within our churches and communities; if we continue to be silent, the powers and principalities of greed and pride will continue to run rampant. If racism is to fall, we must stand both *against* its exploitation and violence and *with* those who suffer under it.

All of this seems daunting and perhaps insurmountable. The stakes created by a racialized society are indeed high—nothing short of life and death. But the only way we can truly battle a spiritual enemy is by first understanding that enemy. Now that we know that racial capitalism seeks to physically and imaginatively kill us, we know we must commit to one another in a corresponding way: physically and imaginatively. As a matter of fact, Christ through the gospel commands us to pursue such commitment when he tells us to love one another. But this kind of truth telling in a world seemingly dominated by the prince of lies requires one more thing. Communities and families committed to anti-violence in a world where might makes right will need this same ingredient. The puzzle needs one final piece. If racial capitalism and its cycle kill by attempting to asphyxiate theological imagination, then we need an imagination with supernatural lungs.

8

The Creative Kingdom

Being a creative sign of the kingdom is a permanent requirement of the church's spirituality and pastoral method.

—Gustavo Gutiérrez, *The God of Life*

Ida B. Wells marshaled all of her creative political energy toward the resistance of lynching. So, too, should we marshal our creative energies against the injustices in our midst. The root of many of these injustices, as I have already pointed out, is greed: the desire to accumulate, which is often accompanied by the desire to dominate. But what might this creativity really look like? I have already outlined the contours of Christian resistance, which are deep economic solidarity, creative anti-violence, and truth telling. But each of these actions points to a deeper imaginative posture: an animating hatred of exploitation and suffering and an animating love for those who have been victimized. Greed is not a benign attitude or action; rather, it kills. Its talons rend flesh, but its tendrils convince us that greed is good and that it is the only way to live. If I don't accumulate for myself, I am told, who will? How will I live? Racial capitalism is the only game in town, so if I don't play it and play it well, how will I keep from falling behind? Relentless profit making is the only way I will survive! Sure, doing so in this world implicates me in systems and processes that chew up the environment and some people more than others, but what choice do I have?

These questions underscore that we need an imagination that can handle the things the Lord has commanded us to do. Yet one of our most profound failures in imagination, particularly in Western theological thought, is our over-spiritualizing of things that Jesus plainly tells us are material. For example, Christ's very first public teaching is this beatitude: "Blessed are the poor in spirit, for theirs is the kingdom of heaven" (Matt. 5:3). Some take these words to mean that the kingdom of God belongs to the humble. Many English versions reflect this interpretation. The Common English Bible says, "Happy are people who are hopeless, because the kingdom of heaven is theirs." The Contemporary English Version says, "God blesses those people who depend only on him. They belong to the kingdom of heaven!" And the Easy-to-Read Version says, "Great blessings belong to those who know they are spiritually in need. God's kingdom belongs to them." It seems that whenever translators want to simplify this text, they make it more spiritual.

John Calvin is one interpreter who takes this line of interpretation, even alongside Jesus's parallel claim in Luke's Gospel: "Blessed are you who are poor" (Luke 6:20). For Calvin, these phrases are metaphors because poverty is obviously an unhappy and cursed state. Matthew, in Calvin's estimation, gives us a better understanding of what Jesus said because by adding the clause "in spirit," he reminds us that the happy poor are those who face adversity but who do so in humility as a result of being disciplined by the cross.[1]

We can't make something more spiritual by removing its materiality. It is much better to press into that materiality, link arms with it, and recognize that the incarnation teaches us that sometimes the material *is* one and the same as the spiritual. Perhaps it's not actually that complicated. In the New Testament, "poor" (*ptōchos* in Greek) means poor, whether it shows up in Matthew 5:3 or Luke 6:20. Gustavo Gutiérrez says it well when he argues that Jesus is saying that "the kingdom of God is promised to those who live in conditions of weakness and oppression and to those also who share their lives out of solidarity with them."[2] Spiritual poverty is then bound up in this understanding: Of course, I need the Lord in order to live this way! Only by the power of the Holy Spirit can we put to death the greed that crouches at our doors, ready to overtake us.

Humility is not merely thinking about ourselves in a particular way. Humility matters insofar as it spurs us to recognize our neediness, to ask for help, and to show material solidarity with the needy. Paul indicates this in Romans 12:16: "Do not be proud, but be willing to associate with people of low position." That is, humility is not merely a disposition. Humility manifests itself in the company we keep and the tasks we complete.

In order to live like this, however, our imaginations need to be sanctified and freed from the strictures of our current political economy. We need to be reminded of what is possible. Perhaps counterintuitively, the way to be reminded of what is possible is to remind ourselves of what Christ has commanded. Instead of responding with the interjection "That's not possible today!" we should respond with the question "Lord, how can you make this possible for me and my community?" As a test of this imaginative work, let's examine one of Jesus's interactions that makes many of us uncomfortable: his conversation with the rich young ruler. By engaging some comments on this conversation made by early church theologians, we find examples of a sanctified imagination.

Clement and the Rich Young Ruler

There are certain biblical passages that American Christians rarely hear preached, because we don't want to think about them. One of them is Jesus's conversation with the rich young ruler. Though the story appears in all four of the canonical Gospels, I'll take a close look at the account in Luke 18:18–30. You'll soon see why.

Luke tells us that someone asks Jesus what he needs to do in order to inherit eternal life. Matthew tells us the questioner is young, Mark just tells us he's a man, but Luke tells us he is a ruler, some kind of official. They all agree that he is rich. Unlike some of the religious leaders' questions that Jesus faces throughout his ministry, this man's question appears genuine, and the Son of God treats it as such. He affirms the man and outlines the commandments that he knows the man knows. The ruler then replies, "All these I have kept since I was a boy" (Luke 18:21). Then Jesus hits the young man where it hurts: "You still lack one thing. Sell everything that you have and give to the poor, and you will have treasure in heaven. Then come, follow me" (v. 22).

In the early third century, Clement of Alexandria, one of the first well-known Christian theologians, interpreted this text in a way most of us are comfortable with today. Jesus seems to be telling the rich young ruler to sell all his stuff, and understanding that Christ's words are not limited to this man, we ask ourselves, "Is he talking to me?" Here is how Clement answers this question:

> "Sell all that you possess": what does this mean? It does not mean, as some superficially suppose, that he should throw away all that he owns and abandon his property. Rather, he is to banish those attitudes toward wealth that permeate his whole life, his desires, interests, and anxiety. These things become the thorns choking the seed of a true life. It is not a great thing or

desirable to be without any wealth, unless it is because we are seeking eternal life. If it were, those who possess nothing— the destitute, the beggars seeking food, and the poor living in the streets—would become the blessed and loved of God, even though they did not know God or God's righteousness.[3]

One can hear the echoes of popular anti-racist thought in Clement's rationalization: racism is about attitudes rather than material redistribution. What matters is how I *feel* about a particular racialized group, so repentance means a changed attitude. I have really repented, I am told, when my friendships and social networks involve more people who are different from me. But as I have iterated over and over in this book, love is not love if it is not material. Clement strips Christ's command of its materiality in order to "make it make sense." Clement is not alone. Subsequent Christian thinkers, reflecting on this text, have made similar conclusions. Augustine distinguishes between "the counsel of perfection" and a command for regular believers: the counsel of perfection is to give up your possessions, whereas the command for regular believers is to just not be overly attached to them.[4] We are comfortable with this spiritualizing move because it doesn't necessarily require sacrifice; rather, it merely requires *openness* to sacrifice if the Lord asks us to do so.

Unfortunately, Jesus, especially in the Gospel of Luke, does not allow us such wiggle room. After expounding on why the Christian shouldn't worry about money or daily needs (in itself an amazing passage), Jesus tells this same crowd of disciples, "Do not be afraid, little flock, for your Father has been pleased to give you the kingdom. Sell your possessions and give to the poor. Provide purses for yourselves that will not wear out, a treasure in heaven that will never fail, where no thief comes near and no moth destroys" (Luke 12:32–33).

The commands to sell one's possessions and to give to the poor are not limited to the rich young ruler. In fact, the only thing the rich young ruler is uniquely asked to do is to sell *everything*. For the rich young ruler, wealth has kept him from following the Lord, so he is called to divest of *all of it*. But instead, he ends up walking away from Jesus "because he was very wealthy" (Luke 18:23).

The general disciple, however, is still told to make a habit of selling and distributing to the poor. In fact, Jesus explains that this is precisely what he means when he commands us to "store up . . . treasures in heaven" (Matt. 6:20): he means that this divine banking system is in the feeding, the sheltering, and the clothing of the poor—that is, Jesus is deeply concerned with the *material*. For Jesus and, as we will soon see, Basil of Caesarea, it is not enough for our attitudes to change. Our habits must change as well. We will not defeat Mammon by merely thinking and believing differently. Within Christian communities, Mammon is defeated, hated, and reviled when solidarity is practiced and the poor are materially cared for. Jesus is, of course, right. We cannot serve both God and Mammon.

Clement concludes that the rich young man hasn't done anything wrong: "Jesus does not accuse the man of having failed to fulfill the law. Instead, he loves him and warmly commends him for his faithfulness."[5] Luke does indeed tell us that Jesus loves the man before he utters his final guidance, but it's a step too far to suggest that Jesus commends him. Instead, in his love, Christ reminds him of what still separates him from eternal life. After all, after this conversation, he will tell his disciples that it is easier for a camel to pass through the eye of a needle than for a rich person to enter the kingdom of God. When the disciples hear that, they rightly understand Jesus to mean that it's impossible. When we hear that, though, we often think it means that it's hard for a rich person to enter the kingdom of God. But it's not just hard to pass a camel through a needle's eye; sometimes, it's hard to get a *thread* through a needle's eye! Jesus is instead saying in this text that riches actively keep the

150

Christian from communion with him, the kingdom of God, and eternal life, and thus the righteous use of riches is to actively give them up. Hence, he concludes the conversation with an "amen" statement: "Truly I tell you, . . . no one who has left home or wife or brothers or sisters or parents or children for the sake of the kingdom of God will fail to receive many times as much in this age, and in the age to come eternal life" (Luke 18:29–30).

Much of the Western tradition sees wealth and riches as a tool and boon to steward; Jesus frames them as enemies to be defeated. In fact, Jesus commends those who leave such things behind for the sake of the kingdom of God. But that leaving is not a naked leaving; the one who does those things is *promised* that they will receive many times that amount *now*, as well as eternal life in the *future*. Rather than viewing these words as a perverse promise of the prosperity gospel (Just sow a seed, give everything you have, and God will make you rich!), we should see them as Jesus's description of the kingdom itself, especially the community that is called to bear witness to it, the church. The prosperity gospel is the perfect example of an attempted marriage between God and Mammon. In all its forms, it encourages the Christian to believe that the two are not rivals but partners. The Christian, we are told, is meant to be rich. This view distorts the Scriptures in order to baptize greed and in so doing reveals itself to be a child of capitalism. In truth, earthly wealth and luxury is not a reward for obedience to God. The Lord promises to provide for our needs, and he promises to do so out of his storehouses, which often happen to be routed *through his people*. That is, when we join the church and give our resources to the poor among us, we gain the resources of the community. We are given gifts, resources we could not have dreamed of, and relationships and connections that enrich our walk with the Lord. But this happens only if we understand that this text is about action, not attitudes. Thankfully, however, we have an excellent guide to help us with this in the teachings of Saint Basil the Great.

Basil and the Rich Young Ruler

Born in Caesarea of Cappadocia, Basil grew up in a prominent Christian family. His family was influential and wealthy. After Basil understood and embraced the gospel, however, he saw that Christ teaches "that a great means of reaching perfection [is] the selling of one's goods, the sharing [of] them with the poor, the giving up of all care for this life, and the refusal to allow the soul to be turned by any sympathy to things of earth."[6] While Basil attempted to live a life obedient to Christ with his own resources, when he became a bishop, he saw a chance to institutionalize that commitment. When he died, Gregory of Nazianzus, his close friend and a fellow Cappadocian Father, regaled the audience of the funeral oration with Basil's good deeds—most prominently, those related to the Basiliad.

The Basiliad was a building complex that Basil created and organized for the care of the needy. The poor and sick had their material needs met free of charge there: food, medical care, clothing, and shelter. Essentially, Basil encouraged the rich to divest themselves of their wealth in order to love their neighbors in need, and this particular effort was funded by both his congregation and the public. While a particular funding structure like that may not be available to all of us today, Basil's Spirit-informed creativity certainly is. Basil founded the Basiliad in an effort to be obedient to Christ. In fact, reflection on Jesus's conversation with the rich young ruler, guided by Basil, gives us a particular example of how our theological and ethical imaginations have been stunted and how Christ actually wants more of us. The existential threats, as I've articulated, are greed in general and racial capitalism in particular. Mammon seeks to keep us in bondage with these two threats. But what weapons do we really have to battle such a seemingly omnipotent foe? Basil's interpretation of Jesus's conversation with the rich man is one such arrow in our quiver.

Basil preached a sermon on Matthew's version of the conversation and addressed it to the rich in his congregation. If they were familiar with the Scriptures, they would have been on edge, as the Scriptures rarely, if ever, have good things to say to or about the rich. In fact, the earliest disciples and early church leaders debated whether the rich *could* be saved. Basil, like Jesus, believed they could, but they would not be able to remain rich while following Jesus.

Whereas Clement argues that the young man has done nothing wrong, Basil is not so sure. He reports himself as saying to his audience: "Although you say that you have never murdered, or committed adultery, or stolen, or borne false witness against another, you make all of this diligence of no account by not adding what follows [that is, you shall love your neighbor as yourself], which is the only way you will be able to enter the Kingdom of God."[7] For Basil, the failure of the young man is fundamentally a failure to love his neighbor as himself, because hoarding wealth is definitionally an act of hate, a lack of love for one's neighbor. That reality should have been obvious to the young ruler. But because he has gotten used to his wealth, it has become "more a part of him than the members of [his] own body" and thus is difficult to get rid of.[8] Basil presses the young man: he does not go away sad because of a wrong attitude. He goes away sad because he is unwilling to pry his hands off material goods.

Basil continues with a blistering catalog of luxuries that he knows his audience enjoys. He's aware of these luxuries because he enjoyed them before coming to know the Lord and giving his own excess to the poor. Yet all these luxuries are demonic distractions: "It is not on account of food or clothing that wealth is sought by most. Rather, some device has been concocted by the devil, suggesting innumerable spending opportunities to the wealthy, so that they pursue unnecessary and worthless things as if they were indispensable, and no amount is sufficient for the expenditures they contrive."⁹

In an ancient agricultural economy, spending more than you needed to spend, saving to give to your children, adding luxuries to your home, and traveling were all unjust when others starved around you. For us today, saving for retirement or college in a society in which both have become more and more expensive appears to be necessary for subsistence. But we, those in the United States, also must remember that millions of people in our midst can only dream about these things. In one study on deep poverty, researchers followed families living on two dollars a day per person in the United States. When asked about their most pressing needs, the parents in these families said they wanted full-time hours, predictable schedules so that consistent childcare would be possible, and maybe $12–13 an hour. Paid time off, retirement, and health insurance rarely came up. For some in the low-wage sector, meeting basic needs is a dream rather than a goal.¹⁰

According to Basil, if we are loving our neighbors as ourselves, we should have no *more* than our neighbors. Said another way, if I determine that I need something I have, I should ensure that all my neighbors also have that thing. Is food a need? I must make sure my neighbor, brother, and sister have it. Is clothing a need? I must make sure my neighbor, brother, and sister have it. Premium health care, high-quality housing, a living wage? All necessities. Through an exegesis of Jesus's words to the young ruler, Basil calls us to think more creatively than neoliberal capitalism would like us to. An economy that grows when we consume will obviously encourage us to continue to consume. Yet we have been called to bear witness to a different kind of economy, one in which we hear Christ's words and do what he says rather than over-spiritualize them.

The Reign of God and Christian Imagination

The three modes of resistance against the demonic cycle of self-interest that created race and fuels racism are these: a commitment to deep economic solidarity, a commitment to consistent and creative anti-violence, and a commitment to truth telling. Such commitments require creativity in a world full of exploitation and lies. Creativity becomes even more essential when we realize that the problem with race and racism lies not merely with thought but also with material exploitation and death. Until we recognize the material effects of what we think and the systems that we participate in, we won't be able to robustly love our neighbors. That much is clear even when we encounter a text such as Luke 18:18–30. Like many other Western interpreters, we quickly over-spiritualize commitments that our Savior intends to be material. In essence, the following is what I am calling us to do when it comes to race: do not over-spiritualize something that is deeply and inextricably material. Race is a category formed and perpetuated to unjustly restrict, oppress, and crush. Best to find ways to actively sap it of its strength.

As I've narrated before, we are in a constant battle against the powers and principalities—spiritual forces that seek to exploit and dominate us. It would be markedly unfair for me to present the options that I have presented without narrating a little bit more of the "how." As I've shown in the previous chapters, the second way that racial capitalism kills is by choking our moral imagination. It tells us that the world looks the way it does because it is supposed to. But not only is the world supposed to look the way it does; it is also impossible to change, so we are told. There will always be persistent economic inequality, and it will likely always be along racial lines. This is one of the refrains that undergirds advocacy for race-based reparations as a tool to remedy the racial wealth gap. But even a robust reparations plan will not solve the problem that we have and the problem that I have narrated. As long as the world is the world, the powers and principalities will have their realm.

The good news is that the world is not all that exists. Christ's first public words in the Gospels of Matthew and Mark are "Repent, for the kingdom of heaven has come near" (Matt. 4:17; cf. Mark 1:15). These words have two parts: a command and an encouragement. The command is to repent and turn from sin toward the Lord and our neighbors. But Christ's call is paired with a revelation. Why should we repent? Because the kingdom of God is at hand and, in fact, closer now than it has ever been. It is among us: in the person of Christ and in the community of his church. The kingdom of God has broken in. Light has pierced the darkness. An alternative logic has asserted itself in a hostile, oppressive, and exploitative world.

I had to read Latin American liberation theology, specifically Antonio González, to be reminded of the theme that saturated Jesus's ministry: the kingdom of God. In fact, this kingdom is what we should have in mind when we speak of "the gospel." The gospel is not merely a particular account of atonement or even a particular theological declaration. What we mean is the good news that we, who have wanted a king, have received the perfect one, God himself. The Romans proclaimed the gospel of their coming emperor. We proclaim the gospel of our King, who has already come and will come again.

This image of the kingdom of God is one of the most prominent images throughout the Scriptures. Richard Hays proposes three normative images to guide how we should understand New Testament ethics: community, cross, and new creation.[11] Each of these images applies to the kingdom of God and dictates the life of the Christian: the church community is to manifest the kingdom in this life, the cross is the logic and shape of the kingdom in this life, and new creation is the power and hope of the kingdom in the life to come. But in order to grasp what this means for the moral imagination needed to resist racial capitalism, we must remind ourselves of what the kingdom of God is. The kingdom of God is *a message, an ethic, and a community.*

The Kingdom Is a Message

The message we need to hear is that the long-awaited King has come in Jesus Christ. In 1 Samuel, the people of God reject their one true King—God—and accept a dynasty of human kings, each of whom dominates and exploits them in a myriad of ways. So as a profoundly creative remedy, one member of the Trinity, the eternal Son of God, takes on flesh and lives a particular human life to give the world the king they have always wanted.

The medieval theologian Anselm of Canterbury wrote the theological classic *Cur Deus homo*, or *Why a God-Man?* In this work, Anselm asks and answers the question of why the Son of God took on flesh. For Anselm, the question is this: Why incarnation and death rather than some other method of salvation? His answer is ultimately that this method is actually maximally fitting, maximally just, and maximally good, the combination of which has made it necessary for God to act in this way. But our response to the incarnation is not one of scholastic inquiry. It is one of wonder. Anselm is right; God could have saved us in another way. He could have saved us with a word. He could have saved us by sending someone else to do his redemptive work. Instead, however, God did it himself and by means of his own death.

The message of the kingdom of God is that the King has finally come. To accept that message is to recognize Christ as king, which is precisely what Paul means when he says that to be saved, one must "declare with [their] mouth, 'Jesus is Lord,' and believe in [their] heart that God raised him from the dead" (Rom. 10:9). To believe that Jesus was raised is to believe that everything he said about life and himself was true, for his resurrection was his vindication. But to say that Jesus is Lord is to say that other lords and gods are not. It is *especially* to say that Mammon is not Lord.

If "Lord" is one of the most important titles for Jesus, it requires that we understand the kingdom in its second sense as well—as an ethic. The sovereign Lord and Master expects those under his rule to live in particular ways!

The Kingdom Is an Ethic

Inextricable from the Christian faith is the fact that God has called us to live in a particular way. Jesus is pretty clear on this point when, ending the Sermon on the Mount, he distinguishes between a wise man who builds his house on a rock and a foolish man who builds his house on sand. What is the difference between the two men? Obedience. The former hears Christ's words and obeys them. The latter hears the same words and does not.

Obedience is one of the primary themes of the Gospel of Matthew: Jesus is the Great Teacher, and we are his disciples. Obedience is the definition of *love* in John's Gospel and epistles (see John 14:15; 1 John 2:3–6). The Christian is to be distinct from the world not merely because of what they believe (the message of the kingdom) but also because of what they do (the ethic of the kingdom). When a person is united to Christ and indwelt by the Holy Spirit, they are equipped to live this alternative life, a life that resists the demonic cycle of self-interest, a life of other-centered mercy, loving one's neighbor as oneself. The kingdom stands ethically against our neoliberal, racialized, and capitalistic society and the ways this society malforms us. The logic of the kingdom of God reminds us that our fellow human beings are not commodities to be exploited or autonomous individuals to be judged. Rather, they are the image of God, to be loved and invited into a new and joyful way of life.

At root, the call to resist racial capitalism and all that it entails is not some added ethical burden that we only read about in obscure, complicated articles and books. The call to resist racial capitalism is the call to obey Christ. It is a call to see each other in the way that God has called us to see each other, a call to live as though Christ has actually died and been raised for us. It is to heed some of my favorite words of Scripture, the words of the author of Hebrews that tell us why the Son of God took on flesh: "[Christ] too shared in [our] humanity so that by his death he might break the power of him who holds the power of death—that is, the devil—and free those who all their lives were held in slavery by their fear of death" (Heb. 2:14–15).

Our political economy restricts our options through fear, whether of reprisal, ridicule, persecution, or death. The death and resurrection of Christ shield us from these fears. In fact, the very purpose of God's salvation through Christ is to make sure that we are never afraid of death again, not because death isn't scary but because death is a defeated enemy. The powers and principalities, though they appear to have a chokehold on the ethical imaginations of everyone around us, are much weaker than they would like us to think. While they present themselves as impassable mountains, the Lord describes his people as threshing sledges: "See, I will make you into a threshing sledge, new and sharp, with many teeth. You will thresh the mountains and crush them, and reduce the hills to chaff. You will winnow them, the wind will pick them up, and a gale will blow them away. But you will rejoice in the LORD and glory in the Holy One of Israel" (Isa. 41:15–16).

We are mountain threshers. The power we have been given in the Holy Spirit is unfathomable. The resources that have been graciously lavished on us by our Savior have been given to us so that we might actually live in the way he has commanded. The ethical call is to, in all things, seek first the kingdom of God and his righteousness. The message of the kingdom reminds us that the kingdom exists. The ethic of the kingdom reminds us to seek it with every fiber of our being.

This ethic, however, is not a merely personal one. It is very simple, especially in Protestant circles, to consider righteousness as an individual endeavor, leading one to think that if one is personally "right with God," then all is well. But the logic of the kingdom of God compels us to think personally, communally, and cosmically. Christ rules you and me, but he also rules his church, the community he has called to live according to his will. When the Scriptures give us descriptions of that community, we do not have the freedom to respond by saying, "I can't do that." Of course, you and I cannot love our enemies and give up our lives for them by force of will. You and I cannot live lives of robust economic solidarity with our brothers and sisters by brute force of will. While we may be able to begin that way, we won't be able to sustain our efforts. But that was never the intention.

After all, we're not the divine Son of God, nor will we ever be! Instead, Jesus, taking on human flesh, also took on a human will, and by actively submitting it to the will of God every moment of his earthly life, he transformed it, revealing to us the way that he seeks to transform us—by his Spirit! If the God of the universe can take on flesh, a phenomenon that appeared to his own people to border on blasphemy, how dare we approach his words and say, "I can't do that!" To say to the commands of Christ "I can't do that" is to misunderstand what the Lord has called us to do. Every "I can't" in response to the Lord's ethical calls must be transformed into a "We can," for the Spirit of God indwells and equips us to live according to the will of God.

The Kingdom Is a Community

When we remember that God has called us as a people, we get a glimpse of what it means to be indefatigable in a world that wears us down. The war that the powers and principalities wage against us is a war of attrition. They will keep attacking us until we get tired and surrender. If they cannot take our lives with their talons, they will settle with taking our imaginations with their tendrils. Our spiritual enemies, those with whom we truly do battle, would like us to forget the Lord's promises and instead focus on the fear and uncertainty of living in a greedy and violent world. But this is precisely why the Lord always works within community. We need to remind each other that though the world is not as it ought to be, it can be, and it will be. It is together that we pray that God's kingdom will come, even here, even now.

The kingdom as a message must be communicated, and as an ethic, it must be lived, but you and I cannot do all this on our own. We have to do it together. Sharing resources requires other people to share with. Love requires relationship. Patience requires people to be patient with. Service requires other people to serve. In fact, the only fruit of the Spirit that is purely personal is self-control—perhaps joy as well. But love, peace, forbearance, kindness, goodness, faithfulness, and gentleness all require communities. As citizens of the kingdom of God, we need a godly community. How do we defeat the lie that political power and violence are the only ways to create systemic change? By living out the logic of the kingdom of God now and realizing that we don't have to wait until the nation or the world gets its act together. We can show it now by the power of the Holy Spirit. In an economy that frames us as endless competitors, we must be communities of coconspirators and colaborers. We must and can, by the power of the Holy Spirit, show the world that there is another way.

Whereas the rest of the world may burn out, the body of Christ has a spring of endless energy and power to tap into. When we stumble, we have others to lift us up. When we fall into sin, we restore one another in repentance and reconciliation. When we suffer financially, we pool our resources together. When one of us rejoices, we all rejoice. When one of us suffers, we all suffer. The images of body, family, and assembly remind us that our identities as followers of Christ are always and ever bound up with one another, regardless of how much neoliberal capitalism may attempt to isolate or individualize us. You will not figure it all out if you just get alone with the Lord.

The kingdom of God is a call to creative rebellion against the powers and principalities. When the world tells us that violence is the only way, we respond with a vision of a future in which there is only Christ-poured-out abundance and a Jesus who has promised us everything we need if we pursue his kingdom first. When the world tells us that actual turning from greed and pride is not possible, we respond with a vision of a world in which all things are made new: you, us, and everything. We respond with a Jesus who heals the sick, cures the blind, raises the dead, and redeems the sinful. The time has come to throw off the talons and tendrils of racial capitalism. Let us do so together!

Epilogue

I do not enjoy talking and writing about race any more than I enjoy talking and writing about violence. But it is imperative. The body of Christ is called to exemplify a different way of thinking and living, and there is perhaps no better space to make that clear than in a racialized society, intent on forming and enforcing categories of violence and exploitation. Amid darkness, the light shines the brightest. The question is whether we are willing to be that people.

The concept of race did not arise as a result of pure reason. It arose to fulfill a particular economic and political purpose: to justify domination and to continue exploitation. This phenomenon explains not all but much of the racialized violence that we have witnessed and continue to witness. Lynchings of Afro-American, Chinese, Italian, and Mexican people are perhaps the most spectacular examples of such violence, though they should be considered alongside the attempted genocide of Native Americans and other forms of racialized oppression in American history. That oppression is an example of what we as human beings can do to one another when we seek to be priests and prophets of Mammon rather than of the kingdom of God.

163

In order to truly be priests of the kingdom of God, as we are each called to be, we need stamina. Racialized capitalism will not be defeated by isolated individuals. But communities that live according to the logic of the kingdom of God have a chance. That chance is not to be measured by global political impact. After all, the goal of the Christian is not to change or to redeem the world. The role of the Christian is to proclaim with their words and with their life that the world has already been changed. The playing field has already been upended. Because Christ has taken on flesh, lived a perfect human life, died, and been raised, those who are called to live in union with him can show the world that the way of life is the way of the cross.

If we view race and racism as parts of a cycle of death, we need to recognize that the Christian church must resist each arm and leg of that cycle. Against the greed that undergirds racialized capitalism's political and economic exploitation, the people of God are called to live lives of radical sharing and generosity. Against the violence that enforces racialized capitalism's conditions, the people of God are called to live lives of robust, consistent, and creative nonviolence. Against the racialized narratives that serve as the ideological ballast for this oppressive political economy, the people of God are called to preach and commit themselves to a more robust framing of humanity, one that evacuates race of its power, first in our own communities and ultimately in the world. In each of these acts of resistance, the Christian is reminded that race is a smoke screen, a powerful construction meant to distract us from and obstruct our view of the flesh-rending talons and throat-crushing tendrils of material domination and exploitation. The Christian is reminded that the gospel is completely and comprehensively anti-greed. The responsibility of the Christian is to seek to break this demonic cycle of self-interest by bearing witness to the fact not only that things are not as they should be but also that Christ has given us a glimpse of how they should be—that we have an opportunity to build communities free of greed, free of domination, and free of exploitation.

I have attempted to cast a vision that can cut through the darkness you have encountered in this book's pages. With the almost overwhelming account of evil that we have seen, we must not forget that the light offered by the kingdom of God is far more brilliant than anything the darkness can muster. While there is ample reason for despair, confusion, frustration, and burnout, the kingdom offers another way: a way of unquenchable joy and hope. Christ has died, is risen, and will come again, and in the meantime, we battle the powers and principalities by the power of his Spirit. These powers will seek to wear us down. But the God we serve will not let us lose. After all, the victory has already been won at the cross.

Malcolm X says that no such thing exists as a turn-the-other-cheek revolution. Jesus begs to differ. The powers and principalities were not defeated by overwhelming force or by out-domination; rather, they were defeated by sacrifice. The Son did not descend with paternalism but with solidarity. The victory won by our Savior has embarrassed the powers and principalities, even the ones that appear so powerful today, because it revealed to them their bankruptcy (though they purport to be rich). Christ calls all who believe in him to share in that victory.

Greed doesn't stand a chance in the face of a people bound and empowered by the trinitarian God. Violence doesn't stand a chance in the face of a people bound and empowered by the trinitarian God. And the lies of race and racism don't stand a chance in the face of a people bound and empowered by the trinitarian God. But race, exploitation, and violence will not die separately. They must die together. The way of resistance that looks not merely to thought but to political economy is a harder way to walk, a way that will require more of us, but it will yield much more lasting results. We will lose nothing in this pursuit that Christ has not promised to restore.

I must mention a final point: I have emphasized the communal in this book because we need Holy Spirit–fueled creativity to do this work. Only you know your particular context and your particular capabilities. I can offer options and creative opportunities, but I am just one man, and this is just one mercifully short book. The kingdom is full of men and women more creative and more intelligent than I am. But we all have the opportunity to invite the world to a new way of life and a new form of community: community suffused with the sanctifying and deifying Spirit of God. Many have never seen such a thing, and that fact is to our shame. We have a hope and a joy that are indescribable, but we still have a responsibility to share that joy and hope, especially because they are so secure.

The sure foundation of our hope and our joy is that we know the end of the story: the end of a story whose climax was the cross. When Christ died and was raised, the powers and principalities were put on notice: the King had arrived, and the King would rule forevermore. Revelation ends not merely with a new world order in which exploitation and domination have no sway or presence. The canon of Scripture ends with a picture of the reign of God *and the saints*. We will sit alongside each other and alongside our exalted Savior. God's intention for humanity will be made visible to all of creation. Love will be the norm throughout the cosmos. We will be, before God, one people. We will see God's face and be as he is. We will not need artificial or natural light because we will be suffused and saturated by divine light. That is the "not yet," but we can taste those joys now. The One seated on the throne says even now, "Behold, I am making everything new" (Rev. 21:5). In union with that One, let's show the world what "new" can be.

Notes

Introduction

1. Ida B. Wells, *Southern Horrors: Lynch Law in All Its Phases* (New York; n.p., 1892), 22–23.

2. Malcolm Foley, "Ought We Kiss the Hand That Smites Us? Black Protestants in the Age of Lynching, 1890–1919" (PhD dissertation: Baylor University, 2021), https://www.proquest.com/dissertations-theses/ought-we-kiss-hand-that-smites-us-black/docview/2622441407/.

3. Martin Luther King Jr., "Where Do We Go From Here?," speech delivered in Atlanta, Georgia, August 16, 1967, Martin Luther King Jr. Research and Education Institute, https://kinginstitute.stanford.edu/where-do-we-go-here/.

4. Oliver Cromwell Cox, *Caste, Class, and Race: A Study in Social Dynamics* (New York: Monthly Review, 1959), 332.

5. Cox, *Caste, Class, and Race*, 333n19.

6. Jonathan Tran, *Asian Americans and the Spirit of Racial Capitalism*, Reflection and Theory in the Study of Religion (New York: Oxford University Press, 2022), 13.

7. Adolph Reed Jr., "Marx, Race and Neoliberalism," *New Labor Forum* 22, no. 1 (2013): 49.

8. For more on this brutal reality, see Terri L. Snyder, *The Power to Die: Slavery and Suicide in British North America* (Chicago: University of Chicago Press, 2015).

9. Charles Seguin and David Rigby, "National Crimes: A New National Data Set of Lynchings in the United States, 1883 to 1941," *Socius: Sociological Research for a Dynamic World* 5 (2019), https://doi.org/10.1177/2378023119841780.

10. Herman Bavinck, *Reformed Ethics*, vol. 1, *Created, Fallen, and Converted Humanity*, ed. John Bolt (Grand Rapids: Baker Academic, 2019), 138–39 (slightly modified).

11. James Henley Thornwell, *The Rights and the Duties of Masters: A Sermon Preached at the Dedication of a Church, Erected in Charleston, SC, for the Benefit and Instruction of the Coloured Population* (Charleston: Walker & James, 1850), 14.

12. Basil the Great, *On Social Justice*, trans. C. Paul Schroeder, Popular Patristics Series 38 (Crestwood, NY: St Vladimir's Seminary Press, 2009), 43.

13. John Chrysostom, *On Wealth and Poverty*, trans. Catharine P. Roth, 2nd ed., Popular Patristics Series 9 (Yonkers, NY: St Vladimir's Seminary Press, 2020), 48.

Chapter 1 How Greed Gave Birth to Race

1. Walter Rodney, *How Europe Underdeveloped Africa* (London: Verso, 2018), 86.

2. Rodney Clapp, *Naming Neoliberalism: Exposing the Spirit of Our Age* (Minneapolis: Fortress, 2021), 7.

3. Adam Smith, *The Wealth of Nations*, ed. Edwin Cannan (New York: Bantam Classic, 2003). See esp. bk. 1, chap. 2.

4. Barrett Strong, "Money (That's What I Want)," on the album *Live and Love*, produced by Berry Gordy, Motown Records, 1976.

5. Bruce Rogers-Vaughn, *Caring for Souls in a Neoliberal Age*, New Approaches to Religion and Power (New York: Palgrave Macmillan, 2019), 17.

6. Rogers-Vaughn, *Caring for Souls*, 109–31.

7. Edward E. Baptist, "Toward a Political Economy of Slave Labor: Hands, Whipping-Machines, and Modern Power," in *Slavery's Capitalism: A New History of American Economic Development*, ed. Sven Beckert and Seth Rockman (Philadelphia: University of Pennsylvania Press, 2016), 31–61.

8. Daina Ramey Berry, "'Broad Is de Road dat Leads ter Death': Human Capital and Enslaved Mortality," in Beckert and Rockman, *Slavery's Capitalism*, 146–47.

9. James H. Sweet, "The Iberian Roots of American Racist Thought," *William and Mary Quarterly* 3, no. 54 (January 1997): 166.

10. Jonathan Tran, *Asian Americans and the Spirit of Racial Capitalism*, Reflection and Theory in the Study of Religion (New York: Oxford University Press, 2022), 18.

11. Tran, *Asian Americans*, 93.

12. Adolph Reed Jr., "Marx, Race and Neoliberalism," *New Labor Forum* 22, no. 1 (2013): 49.

13. Reed, "Marx, Race and Neoliberalism," 49.

14. W. E. B. Du Bois, *Dusk of Dawn: An Essay toward an Autobiography of a Race Concept* (Oxford: Oxford University Press, 2007), 77.

15. Oliver Cromwell Cox, *Caste, Class, and Race: A Study in Social Dynamics* (New York: Monthly Review, 1959), 332.

16. Reed, "Marx, Race and Neoliberalism," 52.

17. Reed, "Marx, Race and Neoliberalism," 53.

18. Richard Rothstein, *The Color of Law: A Forgotten History of How Our Government Segregated America* (New York: Liveright, 2018).

19. Keeanga-Yamahtta Taylor, *Race for Profit: How Banks and the Real Estate Industry Undermined Black Homeownership* (Chapel Hill: University of North Carolina Press, 2019), 5.

20. Taylor, *Race for Profit*, 8.

Chapter 2 The Talons and Tendrils of Racial Capitalism

1. W. E. B. Du Bois, *Black Reconstruction in America, 1860–1880* (New York: Free Press, 1998), 30.

2. Eric Foner, *Reconstruction: America's Unfinished Revolution, 1863–1877*, updated ed., New American Nation Series (New York: HarperPerennial, 2014), 588.

3. For more on the racialization of lynching, see Karlos K. Hill, *Beyond the Rope: The Impact of Lynching on Black Culture and Memory*, Cambridge Studies on the American South (New York: Cambridge University Press, 2016).

4. For some excellent research into this particular number, see Charles Seguin and David Rigby, "National Crimes: A New National Data Set of Lynchings in the United States, 1883 to 1941," *Socius: Sociological Research for a Dynamic World* 5 (2019), https://doi.org/10.1177/2378023119841780.

5. Sutton E. Griggs, *The Hindered Hand; or, The Reign of the Repressionist*, ed. John Cullen Gruesser and Hanna Wallinger (Morgantown: West Virginia University Press, 2017), 93.

6. This account of the death of Jesse Washington comes from *Crisis Magazine*'s reporting of the event. See "Waco Horror: Supplement to the Crisis," *Crisis Magazine*, July 1916, https://library.brown.edu/pdfs/1292363091648500.pdf.

7. Eric Foner, *A Short History of Reconstruction, 1863–1877*, updated ed. (New York: HarperPerennial Modern Classics, 2015), 224.

8. Francis J. Grimké, *Addresses Mainly Personal and Racial*, vol. 1 of *The Works of Francis J. Grimké*, ed. Carter G. Woodson (Washington, DC: Associated Publishers, 1942), 407.

9. Mary L. Dudziak, *Cold War Civil Rights: Race and the Image of American Democracy*, Politics and Society in Twentieth-Century America (Princeton: Princeton University Press, 2000).

10. "K–12 Education: Student Population Has Significantly Diversified, but Many Schools Remain Divided along Racial, Ethnic, and Economic Lines," US Government Accountability Office, June 16, 2022, https://www.gao.gov/products/gao-22-104737.

11. Philip Dray, *At the Hands of Persons Unknown: The Lynching of Black America* (New York: Random House, 2002), 461.

12. Stewart E. Tolnay and E. M. Beck, *A Festival of Violence: An Analysis of Southern Lynchings, 1882–1930* (Urbana: University of Illinois Press, 1995), 239–40.

13. Tolnay and Beck, *Festival of Violence*, 232.

Chapter 3 Lessons of Despair from Francis Grimké and Atticus Haygood

1. Ida B. Wells, *The Light of Truth: Writings of an Anti-lynching Crusader*, ed. Mia Bay, Penguin Classics (New York: Penguin, 2014), 322. All subsequent quotations of Ida B. Wells come from this collection.

2. 56 Cong. Rec. 2151 (1900).

3. Henry Justin Ferry, "Racism and Reunion: A Black Protest by Francis James Grimké," *Journal of Presbyterian History* 50, no. 2 (1972): 77.

4. Francis J. Grimké, *Addresses Mainly Personal and Racial*, vol. 1 of *The Works of Francis J. Grimké*, ed. Carter G. Woodson (Washington, DC: Associated Publishers, 1942), 297–98.

5. Douglas A. Blackmon, *Slavery by Another Name: The Re-enslavement of Black Americans from the Civil War to World War II* (New York: Doubleday, 2008).

6. Grimké, *Addresses Mainly Personal and Racial*, 298.

7. Grimké, *Addresses Mainly Personal and Racial*, 318.

8. Grimké, *Addresses Mainly Personal and Racial*, 333.

9. Malcolm Foley, "'The Only Way to Stop a Mob': Francis Grimké's Biblical Case for Lynching Resistance," in *Every Leaf, Line, and Letter: Evangelicals and the Bible from the 1730s to the Present*, ed. Timothy Larsen (Downers Grove, IL: IVP Academic, 2021). In this essay, I largely look at Grimké's 1906 sermon after the Atlanta race massacre and focus on Grimké's use of the Scriptures. In this book, however, I investigate whether Grimké was right.

10. Grimké, *Addresses Mainly Personal and Racial*, 252.

11. Grimké, *Addresses Mainly Personal and Racial*, 254.

12. Grimké, *Addresses Mainly Personal and Racial*, 255.

13. Ruth Wilson Gilmore, *Golden Gulag: Prisons, Surplus, Crisis, and Opposition in Globalizing California* (Berkeley: University of California Press, 2007), 28.

14. Grimké, *Addresses Mainly Personal and Racial*, 416.

15. Grimké, *Addresses Mainly Personal and Racial*, 417.

16. For more on the fascinating story of the 1920s Klan, especially its use of religion to justify and mobilize its racism, see Kelly J. Baker, *Gospel According to the Klan: The KKK's Appeal to Protestant America, 1915–1930* (Lawrence: University Press of Kansas, 2017).

17. See Emory University's website on its past presidents: https://president.emory.edu/past-presidents/index.html.

18. Atticus G. Haygood, *Our Brother in Black: His Freedom and His Future* (New York; n.p., 1881), 10.

19. Haygood, *Our Brother in Black*, 24.

20. Haygood, *Our Brother in Black*, 12, 35–36, 115.

21. Haygood, *Our Brother in Black*, 112.

22. Atticus G. Haygood, "The Black Shadow in the South," *Forum*, October 1893, 167.

23. "To Be Burned Alive: Henry Smith Captured at Paris, Texas," *New York Times*, February 1, 1893.

24. The above descriptions come from the *New York Times* article that ran on the cover of its February 2, 1893, issue. See "Another Negro Burned: Henry Smith Dies at the Stake—Drawn through the Streets on a Car—Tortured for Nearly an Hour with Hot Irons and Then Burned—Awful Vengeance of a Paris (Texas) Mob," *New York Times*, February 2, 1893.

25. Haygood, "Black Shadow in the South," 168 (emphasis added).

26. Haygood, "Black Shadow in the South," 175.

Chapter 4 Lessons of Resistance from Ida B. Wells

1. Ida B. Wells, *Crusade for Justice: The Autobiography of Ida B. Wells*, ed. Alfreda M. Duster (Chicago: University of Chicago Press, 1991), 47.

2. Paula J. Giddings, *Ida: A Sword among Lions; Ida B. Wells and the Campaign against Lynching* (New York: Amistad, 2009), 182.

3. Wells, *Crusade for Justice*, 52.

4. Giddings, *Ida*, 189.

5. Wells, *Crusade for Justice*, 64.

6. The classic article on intersectionality is the following: Kimberlé Crenshaw, "Mapping the Margins: Intersectionality, Identity Politics, and Violence against Women of Color," *Stanford Law Review* 43, no. 6 (July 1991): 1241–99. Crenshaw focuses on violence against Black women in this article, but her insights about the intersections of race, gender, and class are broadly helpful for any thinking about lynching.

7. Fascinating theoretical work on Black males and their systematic exclusion from intersectional discourse can be found in the following: Tommy J. Curry, *The Man-Not: Race, Class, Genre, and the Dilemmas of Black Manhood* (Philadelphia: Temple University Press, 2017). Curry argues aptly for the distinction of Black male victimization in a way that is neither reducible to complicity in patriarchy, often invoked in these treatments, nor reducible to racism. Controversially and brilliantly, Curry argues that Blackness either negates or transforms what is commonly thought of as gender or sexuality; those categories are recontextualized under racial constructions. Black male sexuality is often glossed as pathological, which is precisely what one sees in the lynching era. Curry's brilliant book highlights how understandings of Black masculinity traffic more in stereotypes than in evidence.

8. Ida B. Wells, *The Light of Truth: Writings of an Anti-lynching Crusader*, ed. Mia Bay, Penguin Classics (New York: Penguin, 2014), 79.

9. Wells, *Light of Truth*, 80.

10. In 1903, Booker T. Washington edited and released a collection of essays written by seven significant Black intellectuals. These essays give a wide range of responses to the "Negro problem," which was framed by Black authors as methods of racial uplift. See Booker T. Washington, ed. *The Negro Problem* (New York: J. Pott, 1903).

11. Wells, *Light of Truth*, 309.

12. Wells, *Light of Truth*, 78.

13. W. E. B. Du Bois, *Black Reconstruction in America, 1860–1880* (1935; repr., New York: Free Press, 1998), 16.

14. Naomi Murakawa, "Ida B. Wells on Racial Criminalization," in *African American Political Thought: A Collected History*, ed. Melvin L. Rogers and Jack Turner (Chicago: University of Chicago Press, 2021), 212–34.

15. Murakawa, "Ida B. Wells on Racial Criminalization," 234.

Chapter 5 Solidarity or Greed?

1. Cyril of Alexandria, *On the Unity of Christ*, trans. John Anthony McGuckin, Popular Patristics Series 13 (Crestwood, NY: St Vladimir's Seminary Press, 2015), 59.

2. St. Athanasius the Great of Alexandria, *On the Incarnation* 54, trans. John Behr (Yonkers, NY: St Vladimir's Seminary Press, 2011), 107.

3. Walter Brueggemann, *Money and Possessions*, Resources for the Use of Scripture in the Church (Louisville: Westminster John Knox, 2016), xix.

4. Brueggemann, *Money and Possessions*, 47. Brueggemann notes that this passage contains seven closely packed infinitive absolutes, grammatically signaling an intensity found nowhere else in the Scriptures.

5. Michael Rhodes and Robby Holt with Brian Fikkert, *Practicing the King's Economy: Honoring Jesus in How We Work, Earn, Spend, Save, and Give* (Grand Rapids: Baker Books, 2018), 161.

6. Some translations (e.g., the NIV) render the Greek *kai* in this verse as "but" rather than "and," but "and" communicates more clearly that the one who stores up things for themselves is precisely the person who is not rich toward God. A "but" suggests that it is possible to be a person who stores up for themselves and rich toward God at the same time. That does not seem to be what Jesus is saying here.

7. Basil the Great, *On Social Justice*, trans. C. Paul Schroeder, Popular Patristics Series 38 (Crestwood, NY: St Vladimir's Seminary Press, 2009), 69.

8. Karl Marx, *Capital*, vol. 1, *A Critique of Political Economy*, ed. Ben Fowkes and David Fernbach, Penguin Classics (New York: Penguin Books, 1981), 873.

9. Thomas L. Friedman, "A Manifesto for the Fast World," *New York Times Magazine*, March 28, 1999, https://www.nytimes.com/1999/03/28/magazine/a-manifesto-for-the-fast-world.html.

10. Westminster Larger Catechism, question 135, https://www.opc.org/lc.html.

Chapter 6 Love or Violence?

1. Notably, the word John uses here is *sphazō*, which means merely to kill by violence. No motive or malice is assumed here, suggesting that anyone who violently kills another fits in this category.

2. Tertullian, *On Idolatry*, in *Ante-Nicene Fathers*, vol. 3, *Latin Christianity: Its Founder, Tertullian*, ed. James Donaldson and Alexander Roberts (New York: Christian Literature, 1885), 73.

3. Antonio González, *God's Reign and the End of Empires* (Miami: Convivium, 2012), 99.

4. Malcolm X, *Malcolm X Speaks: Selected Speeches and Statements*, ed. George Breitman (New York: Grove Weidenfeld, 1990), 4.

5. Malcolm X, *Malcolm X Speaks*, 8.

6. Malcolm X, *Malcolm X Speaks*, 12–13.

7. González, *God's Reign*, 249.

8. González, *God's Reign*, 249–51.

9. Junia Howell and Elizabeth Korver-Glenn, "Appraised: The Persistent Evaluation of White Neighborhoods as More Valuable Than Communities of Color," SocArXiv, last edited November 4, 2022, https://doi.org/10.31235/osf.io/6r5zs.

10. Westminster Larger Catechism, question 136, https://www.opc.org/lc.html.

11. Richard B. Hays, *The Moral Vision of the New Testament: Community, Cross, New Creation; A Contemporary Introduction to New Testament Ethics* (San Francisco: HarperSanFrancisco, 1996), 341 (italics omitted).

12. Hays, *Moral Vision of the New Testament*, 341.

13. Savoy Declaration chap. 24, art. 3, https://reformedstandards.com/british/savoy.html.

14. Second London Baptist Confession, chap. 24, para. 3, https://www.grbc.net/wp-content/uploads/2015/09/The-1689-Baptist-Confession-of-Faith.pdf. This is, in summary, the argument that I make in Malcolm Foley, "Jot and Tittle: The Important Distinctions among the Westminster, Savoy, and Second London Confessions," *Baptist History and Heritage* 52, no. 3 (Fall 2017): 47–64.

15. Confession of Faith in a Mennonite Perspective, art. 22, https://www.mennoniteusa.org/wp-content/uploads/2024/02/Confession-of-Faith-in-a-Mennonite-Perspective.pdf.

16. James H. Cone, *Black Theology and Black Power* (Maryknoll, NY: Orbis Books, 1997), 139.

17. Cone, *Black Theology and Black Power*, 143.

18. James H. Cone, *God of the Oppressed,* rev. ed. (Maryknoll, NY: Orbis Books, 1997), 199.

19. Cone, *God of the Oppressed*, esp. 199–206.

20. Cyril of Alexandria, *On the Unity of Christ*, trans. John Anthony McGuckin, Popular Patristics Series 13 (Crestwood, NY: St Vladimir's Seminary Press, 2015), 102.

21. James H. Cone, *Said I Wasn't Gonna Tell Nobody: The Making of a Black Theologian* (Maryknoll, NY: Orbis Books, 2018), 139.

Chapter 7 Truth or Lies?

1. John Chrysostom, *On Wealth and Poverty*, trans. Catharine P. Roth, 2nd ed., Popular Patristics Series 9 (Yonkers, NY: St Vladimir's Seminary Press, 2020), 51.

Chapter 8 The Creative Kingdom

1. John Calvin, *Commentary on a Harmony of the Evangelists, Matthew, Mark, and Luke*, trans. William Pringle (Grand Rapids: Christian Classics Ethereal Library, n.d.), 1:229, https://ccel.org/ccel/c/calvin/calcom31/cache/calcom31.pdf.

2. Gustavo Gutiérrez, *The God of Life* (Maryknoll, NY: Orbis Books, 1991), 113.

3. Clement of Alexandria, "The Rich Man's Salvation," in *Wealth and Poverty in Early Christianity*, ed. Helen Rhee, Ad Fontes: Early Christian Sources 4 (Minneapolis: Fortress, 2017), 12.

4. Augustine of Hippo, "Letter 157: To Hilarius," in Rhee, *Wealth and Poverty*, 120–29.

5. Clement, "Rich Man's Salvation," 10.

6. Basil the Great against Eustathius of Sebasteia, in *Nicene and Post-Nicene Fathers*, 2nd ser., vol. 8, *Basil: Letters and Select Works*, trans. Blomfield Jackson, ed. Philip Schaff and Henry Wace (Buffalo, NY: Christian Literature, 1895), 263.

7. Basil the Great, *On Social Justice*, trans. C. Paul Schroeder, Popular Patristics Series 38 (Crestwood, NY: St Vladimir's Seminary Press, 2009), 42.

8. Basil, *On Social Justice*, 43.

9. Basil, *On Social Justice*, 44.

10. Kathryn J. Edin and H. Luke Shaefer, *$2.00 a Day: Living on Almost Nothing in America* (Boston: Mariner Books, 2016), 35–63.

11. Richard B. Hays, *The Moral Vision of the New Testament: Community, Cross, New Creation; A Contemporary Introduction to New Testament Ethics* (San Francisco: HarperSanFrancisco, 1996).

THE REVEREND DR. MALCOLM FOLEY (PhD, Baylor University; MDiv, Yale University Divinity School) is a pastor, scholar, and speaker concerned first and foremost with encouraging his brothers and sisters in Christ to live in the joy that Christ has prepared for them. He also serves as special adviser to the president for equity and campus engagement at Baylor University. His writing has been featured by *Christianity Today*, Mere Orthodoxy, and The Anxious Bench. He pastors at Mosaic Waco, an intentionally multicultural church in Waco, Texas. This is his first book.

Connect with Malcolm

 @revdocmalc @MalcolmBFoley